Dear Reader,

"Thy kingdom come . . . on *earth* as in heaven." The earth is our origin and also our final destination – it's the place where the kingdom of God will one day be a reality. After all, the Bible opens with God establishing earth as his garden and closes with him reclaiming it as his home. The resurrection of Jesus' flesh-and-blood body at Easter leaves no doubt that God truly does love his creation, including the earth and all the life it sustains.

Today, for the first time in history, it is possible for millions of people to go through life for long stretches acting as if nature did not exist. Technology allows us to immerse ourselves in an artificial cocoon, detaching ourselves not only from the natural world but also from our fellow human beings, who remain stubbornly non-virtual. And technology cannot bear all the blame. For millions in the cities, nature has become like grass-fed organic beef: a luxury reserved for those who can afford to develop a taste for it.

But the earth is not just ours to enjoy or ignore as we choose. As the contributors to this issue bring home to us, it is *God's* earth. This doesn't mean we should simplistically equate the gospel with ecological activism, as N. T. Wright makes clear (page 16). But it does mean working toward the day when "creation itself will be set free from its bondage to decay and will obtain the freedom of the glory of the children of God" (Rom. 8:21) – the day when "the earth will be full of the knowledge of the Lord as the waters cover the sea" (Isa. 11:9).

To carry out our task on earth, we need to get dirt on our hands. The following pages feature a variety of people who are doing just that. Claudio Oliver tells how his church in Brazil has become a gardening community (page 21). Mary Eubanks recounts her adventures developing drought-resistant varieties of corn for Africa (page 29). Bill McKibben calls us to respond to climate change by replacing hyper-individualism with local economies of sharing (page 10). Other contributors help us catch glimpses of God's revelation in nature through bird watching (8), work on a dairy farm (24), the legacy of John Muir (46), and the painter's vision (54).

Creation naturally includes humankind, made by God as male and female. Last November, religious leaders of many faiths gathered from around the world at the Vatican to reflect on how to promote this truth; the speakers included several Plough writers, as reported on page 6.

Attentive readers may notice we're still experimenting with *Plough Quarterly's* design, including increasing the size of type and adding more art and photography. Now that we've put out four issues, we'd love to know what you think. What would you like to see more of? How can we improve? We look forward to hearing your thoughts.

Warm greetings,

Peter Mommsen
Editor

Photograph by Darius Clement

Readers Respond LETTERS TO THE EDITOR

Receiving the Spirit of Adoption

On Krish Kandiah's "We're All Adopted," Autumn 2014: In the Holocaust, those who risked themselves to save others had nothing in common but one single verifiable trait: they were tenderhearted "mother hens" who took in strays and felt sorry for underdogs of all sorts. They were Christians, atheists, old, young, educated, peasants – the whole cast. Today, I believe that the orphans who need care are often our own grandchildren, or their yuppie orphan friends. It's not always about poverty but also about attention and friendship – being approachable and not buried in a smartphone. *Deanna Clark*

Does God Want Family Breakdown?

On Charles Moore's "Jesus' Surprising Family Values," Winter 2015: What if God is using the breakdown of the family and of the old tribal feelings to help us understand that all men are our brothers? Could it be that we are unable to rightly consider the others as family as long as our own kin take up our affections and our sight? We "naturally" prefer those who look and speak and behave like our kin. Maybe mixing it all up is necessary so that we act as God wants us to, lamentable as this seems to us. "He has made of one blood all those who dwell upon the earth." *Nancy Schmidt*

A Christian Response to Police Shootings

On Eugene Rivers's "Dispatch from Ferguson," Winter 2015: This article summarizes the problem very well, but falls short in offering a solution. I believe the entire Christian body, not just the black churches, needs to step up: to come alongside communities, to mentor, to restore pride and hope. How many of these protesters voted in the last election? How many have attended a PTA meeting? How many have applied for the police academy? The Christian church has failed; we are quick to send aid and missionaries to other countries, yet our local missionaries (Youth for Christ, Young Life, YWAM) and small-community pastors are often the lowest paid, most overworked, and least respected. We need boots-on-the-ground Christian workers who can make a difference by offering hope, light, and love, and we need churches willing to put their money and resources where their faith is! *Mike Wilson*

Is Just War Biblical?

On Ron Sider's "Nonviolence in the Age of ISIS," Winter 2015: You've pointed out that true Christians must be ready to lay down their lives, in the same way soldiers are, if they want to engage in true, nonviolent direct action. That's a difficult thing to ask for, yet it seems like it would be the natural conclusion anyone would come to after reading the Gospels. Why do we Christians find that so difficult? *Timothy Beeman*

The argument as to whether nonviolence or Just War is better is a false argument. The only valid discussion is: Which way is biblical? Can the Just War side produce one single New Testament verse to support their Just War heresy? *Daryl Hartwell*

Flying Babies

On Glenn T. Stanton's "Why Dads Matter," Winter 2015: We were told years ago by our pediatrician that tossing a child in the air helps develop their inner ear and create a strong balance. Those who get tossed in the air do not toss their cookies on windy roads. Our first son was a bit coddled and kept safe and could almost throw up from looking at a map. The second was tossed in the air and had a stomach of iron and a cleaner seat in the car. God's design runs deep. *Jon Stevens*

We welcome letters to the editor. Letters and web comments may be edited for length and clarity, and may be published in any medium. Letters should be sent with the writer's name and address to letters@plough.com.

BREAKING GROUND FOR A RENEWED WORLD

Spring 2015, Number 4

Feature: Earth

Poetry and Story

Reviews

Artists: Piet Mondrian, Wassily Kandinsky, Hannah Marsden, Darvin Atkeson, Diego Rivera, Jason Landsel, Henri Martin, Jean-François Millet, Ivan Shishkin, Lorenzo di Credi, Caspar David Friedrich

WWW.PLOUGH.COM

BREAKING GROUND FOR A RENEWED WORLD

www.plough.com

Plough Quarterly features original stories, ideas, and culture to inspire everyday faith and action. Starting from the conviction that the teachings and example of Jesus can transform and renew our world, we aim to apply them to all aspects of life, seeking common ground with all people of goodwill regardless of creed. The goal of *Plough Quarterly* is to build a living network of readers, contributors, and practitioners so that, in the words of Hebrews, we may "spur one another on toward love and good deeds."

Plough Quarterly is published by Plough, the publishing house of the Bruderhof, an international movement of Christian communities whose members are called to follow Jesus together in the spirit of the Sermon on the Mount and of the first church in Jerusalem, sharing all talents, income, and possessions (Acts 2 and 4). Bruderhof communities, which include both families and single people from a wide range of backgrounds, are located in the United States, England, Germany, Australia, and Paraguay. Visitors are welcome at any time. To learn more about the Bruderhof's faith, history, and daily life, or to find a community near you to arrange a visit, go to *www.bruderhof.com.*

We include contributions in the *Plough Quarterly* which we believe are worthy of our readers' consideration, whether or not we fully agree with them. Views expressed by contributors are their own and do not necessarily reflect the editorial position of Plough or of the Bruderhof communities.

Editors: Peter Mommsen, Sam Hine, Maureen Swinger. Art director: Emily Alexander. Online editor: Erna Albertz.
Contributing editors: Veery Huleatt, Charles Moore, Allen McPherson, Amy McPherson, Bill Wiser.
Founding Editor: Eberhard Arnold (1883–1935)

Plough Quarterly No. 4: Earth
Published by Plough Publishing House, ISBN 978-0-87486-668-1
Copyright © 2015 by Plough Publishing House. All rights reserved.

All Scripture quotations are taken from the New Revised Standard Version unless otherwise noted.

Front cover photograph: Isabel Merritt. Inside front cover: Diego Rivera, *The Corn Harvest, (La cosecha del maiz),* image from Schalkwijk / Art Resource, New York, copyright © 2015 Banco de México Diego Rivera Frida Kahlo Museums Trust, Mexico, D. F. / Artists Rights Society (ARS), New York. Back cover: Ivan Kramskoy, *Beekeeper,* Wikiart (public domain). Painting by Wassily Kandinsky on page 16, image from akg-images, copyright © 2015 Artists Rights Society (ARS), New York.

Editorial Office
PO Box 398
Walden, NY 12586
T: 845.572.3455
info@plough.com

Subscriber Services
PO Box 345
Congers, NY 10920-0345
T: 800.521.8011
subscriptions@plough.com

United Kingdom
Brightling Road
Robertsbridge
TN32 5DR
T: +44(0)1580.883.344

Australia
4188 Gwydir Highway
Elsmore, NSW
2360 Australia
T: +61(0)2.6723.2213

Plough Quarterly (ISSN 2372-2584) is published quarterly by Plough Publishing House, PO Box 398, Walden, NY 12586.
Individual subscription $32 per year in the United States; Canada add $8, other countries add $16.
Application to mail at periodicals postage pricing is pending at Walden, NY and additional mailing offices.
POSTMASTER: Send address changes to *Plough Quarterly,* PO Box 345, Congers, NY 10920-0345.

Featured Books from Plough

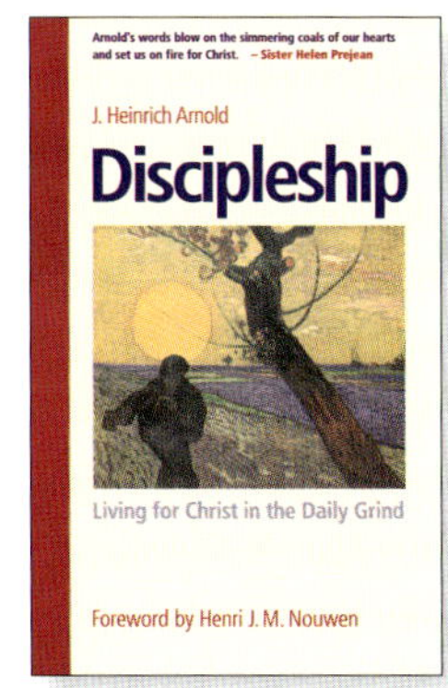

Discipleship: Living for Christ in the Daily Grind *by J. Heinrich Arnold.* Perhaps the hardest thing about following Christ is translating our good intentions into deeds. Sometimes provocative but always encouraging, Arnold guides readers toward leading Christ-like lives amid the stress of modern life. Some chapters offer advice on specific problems; others grapple with broader themes such as world suffering, salvation, and the coming of the kingdom of God.

> "*Discipleship* is a prophetic book in a time in which few people dare to speak unpopular but truly healing words." —Henri J. M. Nouwen

(Don't miss *Homage to a Broken Man,* our new biography of this author, introduced by Eugene Peterson on page 74 of this magazine.)

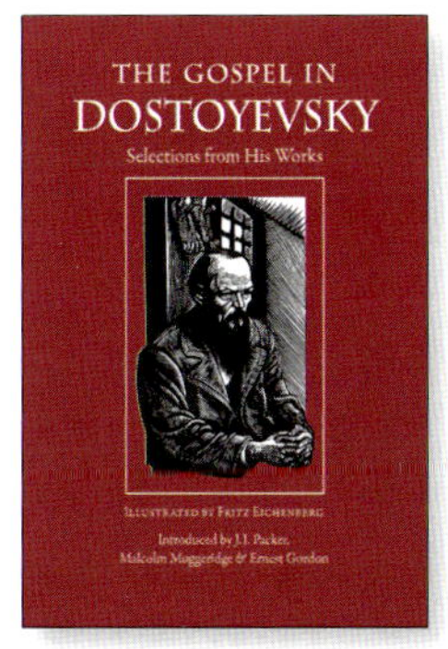

The Gospel in Dostoyevsky: Selections from His Works *Introduced by J. I. Packer, Malcolm Muggeridge, Ernest Gordon; Illustrations by Fritz Eichenberg.* This volume vividly reveals – as none of his novels can on their own – the common thread of the great God-haunted Russian's questioning faith. Newcomers will find in these selections from *The Brothers Karamazov* and his other novels a rich, accessible sampling. Dostoyevsky devotees will be pleased to find some of the writer's deepest, most compelling passages in one volume.

> "Grab it. Read it. And be careful: you may find yourself – as I did – scouring used bookstores for every obscure work of this incomparable writer." —Philip Yancey

Sex, God, and Marriage *by Johann Christoph Arnold; Foreword by Mother Teresa.* Arnold, a pastor for forty years, addresses the pain resulting from broken relationships and the misuse of sexual intimacy. He provides fresh biblical insights into critical issues such as the sacredness of sex, the struggle against temptation, the decision to remain single or to marry, child rearing, homosexuality, divorce and remarriage. Focusing on our personal relationship with God, this book offers hope, healing, and a new beginning to anyone who has known discouragement or failure.

> "Clear, compassionate, uncompromisingly Christian, and straight from (and to) the heart. . . . Pretty close, I think, to what Jesus would say if he were to write a book about sex today – and probably as socially acceptable as he was."
> —Peter Kreeft

The Secret Flower: And Other Stories *by Jane Tyson Clement.* It won't take you long to see why Clement's short stories have become perennial favorites for adults and children alike. Written with a measured beauty that recalls Tolstoy and Tolkien, these tales are rich in allegorical symbolism and infused with the thrill of expectancy – a certainty that God is seeking us, just as we seek him.

> "Clement writes with simplicity and directness, probing insistence, and conviction. One lays down the book in thought, and with thankful heart."
> —*Friends Journal*

www.plough.com

Free access to dozens of e-books for subscribers

Bearing the Image of God

Religious leaders gather to reflect on the dignity of man and woman.

From Wikimedia Commons (public domain)

"Children have a right to grow up in a family with a father and a mother." It's a sign of our strange times that such a statement made headlines around the globe in November 2014, even though Pope Francis was only stating a conviction which most people on the planet share.

The pope was addressing a gathering of religious leaders and scholars from around the world who had been invited to the Vatican to explore what their diverse faith traditions teach about marriage and "the complementarity of man and woman." Several Plough contributors participated in the summit, which included Catholic, Evangelical, Anglican, Pentecostal, Eastern Orthodox, Mormon, Jewish, Muslim, Jain, Buddhist, and Hindu delegates.

Plough author Johann Christoph Arnold and his wife Verena exchange greetings with Pope Francis.

© L'Osservatore Romano

The aim of *Humanum: An International Interreligious Colloquium* was to shore up a vital institution that has experienced decades of decline. Yet despite a host of problems threatening marriage today, the tone remained remarkably upbeat. As participant Russell Moore said, "We stand and speak not with clenched fists or with wringing hands, but with the open hearts of those who have a message and a mission."

Presenters for the most part steered clear of controversy surrounding attempts to redefine marriage, focusing instead on a more fundamental challenge: how religious communities can encourage and support strong marriages and families. Organizers intended the conference to serve as a catalyst for increased cooperation among those who recognize marriage as a cornerstone of healthy families, communities, and societies. Highlights follow.

Jonathan Lord Sacks, former chief rabbi of the United Kingdom: "Science takes things apart to see how they work. Religion puts things together to see what they mean. And that's a way of thinking about culture also. Does it put things together or does it take things apart? What made the traditional family remarkable, a work of high religious art, is what it brought together: sexual drive, physical desire, friendship, companionship, emotional kinship and love, the begetting of children and their protection and care, their early education and induction into an identity and a history.... For a whole variety of reasons... almost everything that marriage once brought together has now been split apart. Sex has been divorced from love, love from commitment, marriage from having children, and having children from responsibility for their care."

Johann Christoph Arnold, Bruderhof pastor and author of Sex, God, and Marriage: "Children and young people desperately need to see role models who prove with their lives that faithful marriage is one of the most wonderful ways one can serve humankind. But married couples standing alone aren't enough. We need strong faith communities to sustain and support

© Corbis Images

them. . . . Marriage is more than a private contract between two people. God did not have in mind merely the personal happiness of separate individuals, but the establishment of God-fearing relationships in a communion of families under his rulership."

Russell Moore, president of the Ethics and Religious Liberty Commission of the Southern Baptist Convention: "All of us in this room share at least one thing in common. We did not spring into existence out of nothing, but each one of us can trace his or her origins back to a man and a woman, a mother and a father. . . . We are not created as "spouse A" and "spouse B," but as man and as woman, and in marriage as husband and as wife, in parenting as mother and as father. Masculinity and femininity are not aspects of the fallen order to be overcome, but are instead part of what God declared from the beginning to be "very good."

Rick Warren, senior pastor of Saddleback Church: "You see, truth is still truth, no matter how many people doubt it. I may deny the law of gravity, but it doesn't change gravity. And just because we break God's laws, does not invalidate them. A lie doesn't become a truth and wrong doesn't become right and evil doesn't become good just because it's popular."

At the close of the event, Eugene and Jacqueline Rivers delivered an affirmation by those assembled, ending with these words: "For marriage is no mere symbol of achievement, but the very foundation – a base from which to build a family and from there a community. For on earth marriage binds us across the ages in the flesh, across families in the flesh, and across the fearful and wonderful divide of man and woman, in the flesh. This is not ours to alter. It is ours, however, to encourage and celebrate."

www.humanum.it

Together on Marriage

Since its launch more than twenty years ago, Evangelicals and Catholics Together has been seeking common ground on a slew of thorny theological issues, from the Lord's Supper to baptism to the Virgin Mary. The group's most recent statement, "The Two Shall Become One Flesh: Reclaiming Marriage," will be published in the March issue of First Things. *The document's signers include Protestants, Catholics, and Anabaptists. Excerpts follow:*

As the most venerable and reliable basis for domestic happiness, marriage is the foundation of a just and stable society. Yet in our times this institution has been gravely weakened by the sexual revolution and the damage it has done to marriage and the family: widespread divorce; the dramatic increase in out-of-wedlock births; the casual acceptance of premarital sex and cohabitation; and a contraceptive mentality which insists that sex has an arbitrary relation to procreation. In this environment, families fragment, the poor suffer, and children are especially vulnerable and at risk. . . .

Christians have too often been silent about biblical teaching on sex, marriage, and family life. Too many have accommodated themselves to the spirit of our age. As Evangelicals and Catholics who speak to and from our various communities of faith, we are committed to setting forth the Christian teaching on marriage. In a few matters, we do not speak with one voice. . . . But on the crucial and fundamental truth that marriage is a stable union based on the complementarity of male and female, we are fully united. . . .

We must find ways to distinguish true marriage from its distortion, and we must do so without abandoning the public square. . . . We encourage our fellow Christians to stand firm in obedience to Christ, for that obedience is the most compassionate service we can offer society. In doing so, we must strive to heal the wounds of a confused and broken culture, to foster human flourishing, and to honor the God who created human beings in his own image, male and female.

www.firstthings.com

Above, birders at the southern tip of Öland, Sweden

BILL WISER

A Spark Bird Lights a Fuse

It was an early spring morning in rural New York. The white blossoms of shadbush graced the hillsides, and underfoot a carpet of green moss contrasted with slender red columbine. But what most caught my attention was a tumble of vigorous notes. The drab olive singer, when I finally located it, seemed impossibly small for such a robust song. With mounting excitement, I studied its field marks, consulted my *Peterson's Field Guide,* and identified it as a ruby-crowned kinglet, the "spark bird" that altered my life forever.

Photograph by Jim Williams

Ruby-crowned kinglet

A spark bird can be of any species. Simply defined, it's the bird that sets alight a lasting love for all things avian. Birders will relate every detail of their spark bird story to anyone who innocently crosses their path. There is no stopping them; just ask my wife.

The writer John Leo once defined birding as "dynamic, addictive, and highly contagious behavior combining hunting skills, aesthetic delight, intellectual analysis, and the dreamy withdrawal from normal life, especially during spring migration. . . . There's an awful lot of adventure in it. It allows grownups to do things they thought they had put behind them when they grew up, like sloshing around in the mud and getting up in the middle of the night and going out looking for things."

I readily admit to all this, and treasure every adventure along the way. An undoubted high point involved taking a team of eleven-year-olds to the *World Series of Birding* competition and fundraiser in May 1993. For nineteen hours we crisscrossed Cape May County, New Jersey, logging one hundred and fifteen species. I will never forget the sight of some three thousand red knots feeding on horseshoe crab eggs, stocking up on protein before embarking on the last leg of their nine-thousand-mile journey from the southern tip of South America to their breeding grounds in the Arctic. We were awed spectators of this timeless drama, now threatened by the precipitous decline of this shorebird's North American population.

That day led to invitations to offer workshops on environmental education. In one of these, I described how adults can foster children's environmental *awareness,* shaping it into *appreciation* for the intricacy and fragility of the web of life. Add the involvement of schools or civic groups, and appreciation leads to *action.* Birding draws participants into a range of habitats, providing a remarkably visible interface with the natural world; this "Triple A" framework transforms something fun and exciting into an effective tool for educating children about the environment.[1]

A workshop participant from Beijing, radio journalist and environmental leader Wang Yongchen, related her own spark bird story. She told of a boy in rural China who killed an owl and triumphantly brought the dead bird to school. His teacher explained to the boy how owls benefit his village by reducing rodent damage to crops. The lesson stuck: when the child grew up and became principal of a

Photograph by Pontus Åkerholm / www.flickr.com/photos/pakerholm

primary school, he initiated weekly bird study classes, helped the children build nesting boxes, and set up a primitive rehabilitation hospital for injured birds. The local avian population slowly recovered from near destruction deliberately set in motion by the misguided policies of China's Communist government under Mao Zedong. And as nature's balance was restored, the villagers reported that crop yields increased.[2]

When Yongchen visited the school, she heard bird song, notably absent elsewhere across rural China. Her subsequent radio broadcast generated a flood of letters, raising environmental awareness and advocacy throughout China. Awareness, appreciation, action.

Raising environmental consciousness does not require deep knowledge. Rather, I invite parents, educators, and mentors to join the children in the high drama of discovery, as child and adult identify a plant, bird, or insect and learn about its unique place within the web of life.

Seven years ago, a group of home-schooled children that I mentor in New South Wales, Australia, envisioned a "nature paddock" in which an array of newly planted flora would attract a diverse range of fauna. Adults smiled, looking at the vacant lot; undaunted, the children raised funds, then bought and planted trees and shrubs.

Year by year, the children's vision is becoming reality – far more successfully than we had hoped. Today, native birds and other creatures that had abandoned the area have returned, to the delight of the children, who meticulously record each arrival with detailed notes, sketches, and paintings. Once the tinder has been ignited, the range and scope of action are limitless, no matter how tiny the initial spark.

Bill Wiser lives in Elsmore, New South Wales, Australia.

1 "Bills and Feathers," 1994 Nature Educator of the Year – Runner up, in *Teaching Nature: Ideas that Work!*, The Roger Tory Peterson Institute of Natural History.

2 Bill Wiser, "Global Thought, Local Action," *A Bird's-Eye View*, Vol. 4, No. 4 (November 1996), American Birding Association.

Photograph by Bill Dalton

Mixed migration: red knots, dunlins, and ruddy turnstones

Ivan Shishkin, *Birch Grove*

All Ivan Shishkin art from WikiArt (public domain)

Can Anything Good Come from Climate Change?

INTERVIEW WITH BILL MCKIBBEN

It's time to build communities, push for change, study the Bible, and take the kids camping.

Inspired by his love of the Adirondack Mountains, Bill McKibben was one of the first to raise the alarm about climate change twenty-six years ago, when few realized it might be a threat. Last September, he and fellow activists at 350.org helped to organize the People's Climate March, which brought 400,000 people to New York City and included 2,600 events in solidarity around the world. McKibben is the author of more than a dozen books, teaches at Middlebury College, and keeps bees.

Plough: *You've been warning about climate change ever since the 1989 release of your book* The End of Nature. *For those who haven't stayed abreast of the latest developments, what's important to know?*

Bill McKibben: This last year we learned that the great West Antarctic ice sheet has begun an irreversible melt; and the waters of our ocean planet are rapidly acidifying. Summer sea ice in the Arctic is largely a thing of the past. When the biggest features on earth are being remade in just a matter of years, that is a bad sign. And of course we can see it close up in the endless siege of extreme weather – drought, flood, storm, and the other phenomena we once called biblical.

Your book Eaarth *delivers a heavy dose of apocalyptic warnings; you've even described it as "grim." Can anything good come out of climate change?*

Sure. If we build the movement that breaks the power of the fossil fuel industry and allows us to bring renewable energy and efficiency to scale in time, then our future is sweet: local, democratic power available everywhere with little pollution and with none of the gross inequality that comes when a few people own the sand dunes and coal mines that everyone else depends on.

Ivan Shishkin, *Dam*

Building Communities

You've written that "when people ask me where they should move to be safe from climate change, I always tell them, 'Any place with a strong community.'" How do we build those places?

Though we pay a lot of lip service to "community," real community is pretty much the opposite of what we've specialized in for the last seventy-five years. We live in the era of hyper-individualism and have taken it to an extreme that no other society has ever managed before. So we know what not to do. For instance, don't build big houses far apart from each other. Not only do they waste insane amounts of energy, they also make it very difficult to live in the way that human beings always have lived – in close contact with each other.

Anyone who has tried community knows that there are some all-too-human roadblocks to living together. How will we learn the new habits needed for this way of life?

We need to depend on our neighbors for something real. For Americans in the last fifty years, neighbors have been largely optional. For social primates, which humans are, that's a very weird situation, and ultimately a depressing one. Today the average American has half as many close friends as his counterpart five decades ago. You asked before if there was good news about climate change; I suppose, in one sense, there is. We will need to pull together.

Here at Middlebury College where I teach, I tell the students that college will likely be the only chance they'll ever get to live as most human beings have always lived: in close physical and emotional proximity to a lot of other people. Of course, sometimes that's a pain in the butt, but mostly it's satisfying – after all, plenty of people will say that their college years were the best in their life. The irony, of course, is that the goal of most higher education is to prepare students to earn enough money so that they never have to live that way again. But this isn't inevitable. There are other possibilities.

In your book Deep Economy, *you describe what some of those possibilities might look like, starting with the local grocery store.*

Localness is where we are heading. For the past century or two, with cheap fossil fuel as the wind in our sails, we have thrown out ever longer supply lines reaching all over the world. It makes sense to share recipes over the internet; it doesn't make sense to ship the ingredients halfway around the world when we can grow them here.

The good news is that change is already happening. According to a recent USDA report, the number of farms in America is growing instead of shrinking for the first time in 150 years. Who are these new farmers? Most are young people taking over small farms to grow food for their neighbors.

Ivan Shishkin, *Mast Tree Grove*

You've pointed out that it's too late for lifestyle environmentalism – driving a Prius, installing efficient light bulbs – to save earth as we've known it. What kind of changes should individuals be making?

We need to build movements that are themselves a form of community.

We *should* change our light bulbs – I have, twice, and the new LEDs are great. But I don't try to fool myself that that's enough. Global warming is a structural and systemic problem. Until now, we've allowed ourselves to pour carbon for free into the atmosphere – to use the heavens as an open sewer. That needs to change. And for real change to happen, the most important thing that we as individuals can do is to stop being individuals for a while, and to join together and organize!

Pushing for Change

In 1971, Richard John Neuhaus wrote a book critiquing the then-fledgling environmental movement, provocatively titled In Defense of People. *Can green activism distract us from our obligations to people – say, feeding hungry children?*

To me it seems the reverse. People fighting climate change are doing it in the company of the poorest people on earth, who realize that their very existence is at stake. And in my experience the same people who pooh-pooh whales and redwoods usually don't have much sympathy for the victims of injustice either.

What got me passionate about climate change was a trip I made some years ago to Bangladesh. While I was there, they had their first big outbreak of dengue fever, a mosquito-borne disease that is spreading in the developing world because of rising global temperatures. It's a horrible sickness, with no vaccine or effective medication available – in its most extreme form, it results in internal and external bleeding, and sometimes death.

I was spending a lot of time in the slums, so eventually I got bit by the wrong mosquito and got sick myself, as sick as I've ever been. Since my health had been strong beforehand, I didn't die. But lots of people did, especially children and old people. Standing in that Bangladeshi hospital ward looking at the rows of shivering patients, I knew these people did nothing to deserve this.

Bangladesh has a population of over 150 million, but their contribution to climate change is basically nil – very few of them have cars or electricity. By contrast, the United States has 4 percent of the world's population, yet we produce 25 percent of the world's carbon dioxide.

My point is: fighting climate change is about ensuring that hungry children have something to eat – after all, the people who are being hardest hit are subsistence farmers in developing countries. And it's about protecting children from dying in human-caused epidemics.

Climate change has become a partisan dividing line between left and right. Does that trouble you?

It's not a left–right issue; it's become a money issue. In fact, environmentalists working on climate change are the truest kind of conservatives. I defy you to name a more radical, anticonservative act than changing the chemistry of the atmosphere and just waiting to see what happens – especially once scientists have told you what's going to happen, and then you see it actually starting to happen. All that environmentalists are saying is, "Can't we have a world that resembles, at least in some ways, the world that all humans over the last ten thousand years have called home?" That's not radical; it's conservative. But money means power, and the fossil-fuel industry is the richest industry on earth.

Ivan Shishkin, *In the Wild North*

Still, aren't we individually also part of the problem?

Look, we are all enmeshed in a fossil-fuel economy. But do you care, when you turn on the light switch, whether your power is coming from a solar panel or a coal mine? The only people who have a strong opinion on this question are people who own coal mines. That's why they spend hundreds of millions of dollars gaming our political system to make sure that they stay the richest people on the planet.

But this doesn't mean things can't change. There were days in summer 2014 when Germany generated 80 percent of its power from the sun. The Germans don't have much sun, but they do have political will.

The People's Climate March last September was massive, with indigenous communities, college students, union members, and scientists in white lab coats all marching together. What comes next?

We need to build movements that are themselves a form of community. We have enormous issues to address. In order to address them, we need strong movements of people demanding action.

The most moving Sunday morning I've spent in many years was not in a church but in a Washington, DC, jail in 2011, after I was arrested with other marchers in front of the White House. I imagine more of us will need to go to jail before the decade is out.

Readers of your book Oil and Honey *know that you love living close to the land, and would rather be beekeeping in Vermont than hotel-hopping around the country. Is the activist life actually – to use a loaded word – sustainable?*

No. If everyone was on an airplane all the time trying to build a movement, the carbon would overwhelm us all. That's why we've tried to build 350.org with as few moving parts as possible, a movement that works locally in thousands of places and yet can come together as one when the occasion demands. I'm trying to leave the frequent flyer club – Skype is a blessed invention in my opinion.

Can the battle be won?

I don't know if we're going to win – we've waited a long time to get started. But I do know we're going to fight, and that it's the fight of our time.

What fascinates me about Gandhi and Martin Luther King Jr. is not only the clarity of their moral visions, but also the power of their tactical acumen. These two qualities are not unrelated. Their insight from the Sermon on the Mount – that one heaps coals on the head of one's adversary when one returns kindness for enmity – is invaluable. It underlay the fall of the British Empire in India and the fall of Jim Crow in the United States.

Ivan Shishkin, *Twilight after Sunset*

For Gandhi and King, time was on their side.

That highlights the special challenge of climate change. Unlike past struggles, it's a timed test – if we don't change our ways quickly, it won't matter. In this case, God has given us a blue exam book, and when a certain amount of time has passed, we have to put our pencils down. It reminds me of the great old hymn:

Once to every man and nation,
comes the moment to decide,
In the strife of truth with falsehood,
for the good or evil side;
Some great cause, some great decision,
offering each the bloom or blight,
And the choice goes by forever,
'twixt that darkness and that light.

In much of life, fortunately, we have multiple chances to decide and redeem ourselves, and the choice does not go by forever. But in the case of climate change, the hymn has it exactly right. If we don't settle this soon, it will settle us.

That sounds alarmist. Are you calling for a radical change of lifestyle?

Let me answer that in two parts. First, there's definitely a lack in modern society that leaves us less happy than we might otherwise be, so it's important to think about other ways of living. Equally important – probably more so – is the fact that we just cannot go on in the way we have been. The temperature of the planet is rising sharply; 2014 was the hottest year on record. We need to figure out some different arrangements quickly. Do they have to be "radical?" Not necessarily, but they do have to be thorough. We'll need some dramatic moves.

Who Is My Neighbor?

You spoke earlier about hyper-individualism and consumerist behavior. Perhaps the more accurate words would be "selfishness" and "materialism."

One of the powerful stories for our time is the story of the rich young man whom Jesus tells to sell what he has and give it to the poor (Mark 10:17-30). The Gospel says: "He went away sorrowful; for he had great possessions." Chances are his list of possessions was not as long as the list that goes with being an average middle-class American. Many of us go away sorrowful from what we know we are called to because we have great possessions with which we are reluctant to part.

Where do Christians in particular need to step it up?

We are charged to watch out for the least among us. That should be our top priority. Yet in the United States, laws are being rewritten to benefit the most privileged among us, and golden calves are being erected in honor of mammon.

The very first chapters of the Bible teach us about the good world we've been given and how we are commissioned to take care of it in God's stead. No discussion about dominion theology is necessary. At this point in history, we clearly have our thumb on the scale of nature, and we're doing a terrible job of stewardship. We're like the bad babysitter who takes the two-year-old out to get a tattoo.

Ivan Shishkin, *Wildflowers near the Water*

Christians are called to love their neighbors as themselves, so climate change strikes at the heart of our integrity. Our high-consumption way of life is drowning, sickening, and impoverishing our neighbors. No number of mission trips can make good the damage.

You're currently teaching a course on "Stories from the Bible." Are there any stories that strike you as especially relevant now?

I love the story of Job, particularly God's speech from the whirlwind at the end of the book. This passage is the best piece of nature writing in the Western tradition – a beautiful tour of the crunchy, earthy, buzzing, cruel, magnificent world of creation, filled with its animals, plants, organisms, and natural forces. The Lord tells Job: You are not the center of everything. You are a small part of something very big. So stop whining.

There's no calling higher than taking kids out camping.

Our problem today is that we are rewriting that story. When God asked Job, "Can you tell the proud waves 'Here you shall go and no further'?" Job had to say "No, that's your job." But in our time, we are able to figure out how high the sea is going to rise and how hard the wind is going to blow. For the first time in human history, we are able to just spit in God's face if we want to. That's a bad, sad place to be.

Job's response is to fall down before God, overwhelmed with awe for creation and the Creator. How can we reclaim that sense of wonder?

One way is to get people out into nature. The world is still a beautiful place, even if we've damaged it some. There is no calling higher than taking kids out for a camping trip, letting them see the Milky Way, helping them understand what a big and beautiful thing creation is.

Interviews by Peter Mommsen and Sam Hine on January 16, 2015 and December 20, 2014. Watch the video version at www.plough.com.

Wassily Kandinsky, *Improvisation 9*, oil on canvas, Staatsgalerie, Stuttgart

Jesus Is Coming – Plant a Tree!

N.T. WRIGHT

We have declared, in the Nicene Creed, that Jesus Christ "will come again in glory to judge the living and the dead, and his kingdom shall have no end," but neither mainline Catholic nor mainline Protestant theology has explored what exactly we mean by all that, and we have left a vacuum to be filled by various kinds of dualism. In particular, Western

Christianity has allowed itself to embrace that dualism whereby the ultimate destiny of God's people is heaven, seen as a place detached from earth, so that the aim of Christianity as a whole, and of conversion, justification, sanctification, and salvation, is seen in terms of leaving earth behind and going home to a place called heaven.

So powerful is this theme in a great deal of popular preaching, liturgy, and hymnography that it comes as a shock to many people to be told that this is simply not how the earliest Christians saw things. For the early Christians, the resurrection of Jesus launched God's new creation upon the world, beginning to fulfill the prayer Jesus taught his followers, that God's kingdom would come "on earth as in heaven" (Matt. 6:10), and anticipating the "new heavens and a new earth" (Isa. 65:17, 66:22; 2 Pet. 3:13; Rev. 21:1) promised by Isaiah and again in the New Testament. From this point of view, as I have often said (though the phrase is not original to me), heaven is undoubtedly important, but it's not the end of the world. The early Christians were not very interested, in the way our world has been interested, in what happens to people immediately after they die. They were extremely interested in a topic many Western Christians in the last few years have forgotten about altogether, namely the final new creation, new heavens and new earth joined together, and the resurrection of the body that will create new human beings to live in that new world.

The question of how you think about the ultimate future has an obvious direct impact on how you think about the task of the church in the present time. To put it crudely and at the risk of caricaturing: if you suppose that the present world of space, time, and matter is a thoroughly bad thing, then the task is to escape from this world and enable as many others to do so as possible. If you go that route, you will most likely end up in some form of gnosticism, and the gnostic has no interest in improving the lot of human beings, or the state of the physical universe, in the present time. Why wallpaper the house if it's going to be knocked down tomorrow?

At the opposite end of the spectrum, some theologians have been so impressed with the presence and activity of God in the present world that they have supposed God wants simply to go on working at it as it is, to go on improving it until eventually it becomes the perfect place he has in mind. From this point of view, the task of the Christian is to work at programs of social and cultural improvement, including care for the natural environment, so that God's kingdom will come on earth through an almost evolutionary process, as in Teilhard de Chardin, or at least until human hard work in the present world attains the result God ultimately intends. . . .

I first ran into the problem I'm addressing here during a weekend of lectures in Thunder Bay, Ontario, in (I think) 1982 or 1983. I was working in Montreal at the time and was asked to talk about Jesus in historical context. . . . To my surprise, the main question people had in mind was not the meaning of the parables or of the cross or the incarnation itself, but questions of ecology: some people in the church had been saying that there was no point in worrying about the trees and acid rain, the rivers and lakes and water pollution, or climate change in relation to crops and harvests, because Jesus was coming back soon and Armageddon would

N. T. Wright, whose writings on Jesus and Paul have established him as a leading New Testament scholar, is the former Bishop of Durham in the Church of England. This article is taken from his recent book Surprised by Scripture: Engaging Contemporary Issues *(HarperOne, 2014). Used by permission of the publisher.*

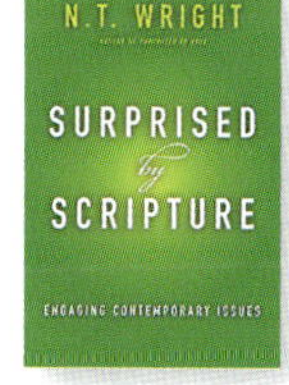

destroy the present world. Not only was there no point in being concerned about the state of the ecosystem; it was actually unspiritual to do so, a form of worldliness that distracted from the real task of the gospel, which was the saving and nurturing of souls for a spiritual eternity. I can't now remember what sort of answers I gave to these questions, but the questions themselves have stayed with me.

. . . . .

It is striking how the earliest Christians, like mainstream rabbis of the period, clung to the twin doctrines of creation and judgment: God made the world and made it good, and one day he will come and sort it all out. Take away the goodness of creation, and you have a judgment where the world is thrown away as so much garbage, leaving us sitting on a disembodied cloud playing disembodied harps. Take away judgment, and you have this world rumbling on with no hope except the pantheist one of endless cycles of being and history. Put creation and judgment together, and you get new heavens and new earth, created not *ex nihilo* but *ex vetere,* not out of nothing but out of the old one, the existing one.

Heaven is important, but it's not the end of the world.

And the model for that is of course the resurrection of Jesus, who didn't leave his body behind in the tomb and grow a new one but whose body, dead and buried, was raised to life three days later and recognized by the marks left by the nails and the spear. There is a whole world of eschatological understanding in the resurrection narratives, not least John's insistence that Easter day is the first day of the week; John, so rooted in creational theology, knows exactly what he is doing. Easter is the beginning of God's new creation. We don't have to wait. It has already burst in. And the whole point of John 20 and 21 is that we who believe in Jesus are to become, in the power of his spirit, not only beneficiaries of that new creation but also agents.

I end with an extraordinary verse, 1 Corinthians 15:58: "So, my dear family, be firmly unshakable, always full to overflowing with the Lord's work. In the Lord, as you know, the work you're doing will not be worthless." Now what is that exhortation doing at the end of a chapter on resurrection? If we were to take the normal Western view of life after death, a long chapter on resurrection might end with something like this: "Therefore, my beloved, lift up your head and wait for the wonderful hope that is coming to you eventually." But for Paul, as is clear throughout 1 Corinthians, *the resurrection means that what you do in the present matters into God's future.* That is so for ethics, not least sexual ethics, as in 1 Corinthians 6. But it is also so for everything else. The resurrection, God's recreation of his wonderful world, which began with the resurrection of Jesus and continues mysteriously as God's people live in the risen Christ and in the power of his spirit, means that what we do in Christ and by the Spirit in the present is not wasted. It will last and be enhanced in God's new world.

I have no idea precisely what this means. I do not know how the painting an artist paints today in prayer and wisdom will find a place in God's new world. I don't know what musical instruments we will have to play Bach, though I'm sure Bach's music will be there. I don't know how my planting a tree today will relate to the wonderful trees that will be in God's recreated world. I don't know how my work for justice for the poor, for remission of global debts, will reappear in that new world. But I know that God's new world of justice and joy, of hope for the whole earth, was launched when Jesus came out of the tomb on Easter morning: I know he calls me and you to live in him and by the power of his spirit, and so to be new-creation people here and now, giving birth to signs and symbols of the kingdom on earth as in heaven. The resurrection of Jesus and the gift of the Spirit mean that we are called to bring forth real and effective signs of God's renewed creation even in the midst of the present age. Not to do so is at best to put ourselves in the position of those Second Temple Jews who believed they had to wait passively for God to act – when God *has* acted in Jesus to inaugurate his kingdom on earth as in heaven. At worst, not to bring forth works and signs of renewal in God's creation is to collude, as gnosticism always does, with the forces of sin and death.

This doesn't mean that we are called to build the kingdom by our own efforts, or even with the help of the Spirit. The final kingdom, when it comes, will be the free gift of God, a massive act of grace and new creation. But we are called to build for the kingdom. Like craftsmen working on a great cathedral, we have each been given instructions about the particular stone we are to spend our lives carving, without knowing or being able to guess where it will take its place within the grand design. We are assured, by the words of Paul and by Jesus' resurrection as the launch of that new creation, that the work we do is not in vain. That says it all. That is the mandate we need for every act of justice and mercy, every program of ecology, every effort to reflect God's wise stewardly image into his creation. In the new creation, the ancient human mandate to look after the garden is dramatically reaffirmed – another point we could draw out of John 20 were there time. The resurrection of Jesus is the reaffirmation of the goodness of creation, and the gift of the Spirit is there to make us the fully human beings we were supposed to be, precisely so that we can fulfill that mandate at last. What are we waiting for? Jesus is coming. Let's go and plant those trees.

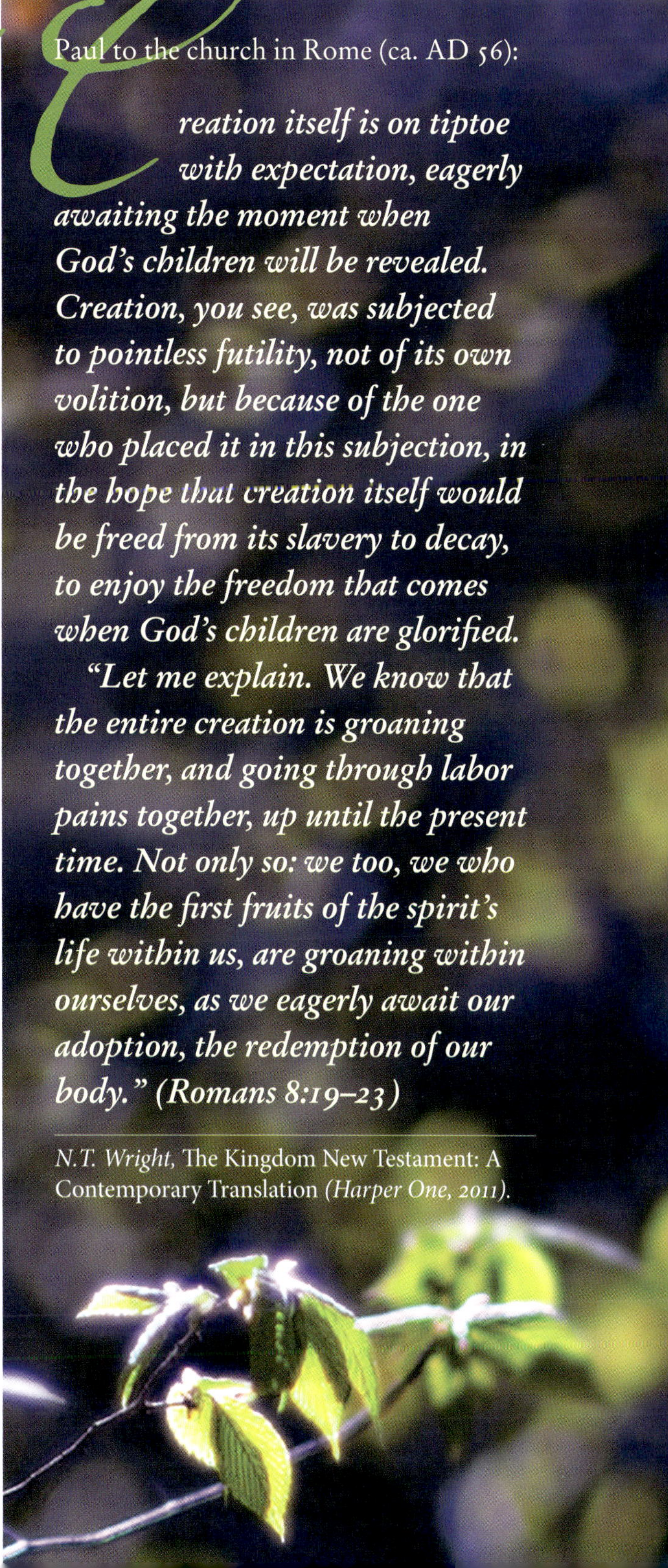

Paul to the church in Rome (ca. AD 56):

"Creation itself is on tiptoe with expectation, eagerly awaiting the moment when God's children will be revealed. Creation, you see, was subjected to pointless futility, not of its own volition, but because of the one who placed it in this subjection, in the hope that creation itself would be freed from its slavery to decay, to enjoy the freedom that comes when God's children are glorified.

"Let me explain. We know that the entire creation is groaning together, and going through labor pains together, up until the present time. Not only so: we too, we who have the first fruits of the spirit's life within us, are groaning within ourselves, as we eagerly await our adoption, the redemption of our body." (Romans 8:19–23)

N.T. Wright, The Kingdom New Testament: A Contemporary Translation *(Harper One, 2011).*

Photograph by Clare Stober

Henri Martin, *Summer*

From WikiArt (public domain)

Our Garden, God's Garden

Why the Gospel Calls Us to Life in Community

EBERHARD ARNOLD

ALL LIFE – including the variety we see in nature – is a parable of the future community of the kingdom of God. Just as the air surrounds us, or as a blowing wind engulfs us, we need to be immersed in the blowing Spirit, who unites and renews everything. And just as water washes and cleanses us every day, so in the symbol of baptism we witness to our purification from everything that is of death. This "burial" in water, which is once and for all, signifies a complete break from the status quo; it is a vow of mortal enmity toward the evil in us and around us. Similarly, the lifting out of the water proclaims resurrection in vivid imagery and in unforgettable clarity.

The resurrection we see in nature is just the same: after the dying of autumn and winter comes the blossoming of spring and the fruit-bearing of summer; after seedtime comes harvest. The whole course of human history, from humankind's origins to its fulfillment at the end of time, is symbolized by the cycle of nature.

WE LOVE THE BODY because it is a consecrated dwelling place of the Spirit. We love the soil because God's spirit spoke and created the earth, and because he called it out of its uncultivated natural state so that it might be cultivated by the communal work of human beings. We love physical work – the work of muscle and hand – and we love the craftsman's art, in which the spirit guides the hand. In the way spirit and hand work together and through each other, we see the mystery of community.

We love the activity of mind and spirit, too: the richness of all the creative arts and the exploration of the intellectual and spiritual interrelationships in history and in humanity's destiny of peace. Whatever our work, we must recognize and do the will of God in it.

God – the creative Spirit – has formed nature, and he has entrusted the earth to us, his sons and daughters, as an inheritance but also as a task: our garden must become his garden, and our work must further his kingdom.

From Eberhard Arnold, Why We Live in Community, *with Thomas Merton (Plough, 1995).*

LETTER FROM BRAZIL

Becoming a Rooted Church

CLAUDIO OLIVER

Casa da Videira ("House of the Vine") is a collective of families in Curitiba, Brazil, dedicated to "following the steps of Jesus." Their work in organic gardening, waste management, and fair trade is inspired by Jesus, the first Christians, and guides as diverse as Thomas Aquinas, William Booth, Leo Tolstoy, Eberhard Arnold, and Vandana Shiva. While the group gladly receives people of varying commitment and beliefs, major decisions are made by those committed to Christ and a scriptural basis. Supported through donations and crowdfunding, they depend on prayer while working towards financially supporting themselves by selling traditional bread and groceries as well as soap made from recycled vegetable oil. Claudio Oliver, the community's pastor (pictured above), reports:

Our journey has been rooted in scripture, culture, and agriculture. One of our community's most important values is to "embrace contingency" – to welcome each encounter God sends us, just as Jesus taught in the story of the Good Samaritan, who helped the wounded man he found lying on the Jericho road. This is far more important than any strategic planning. Rather than attempting to determine where we are going, we must know with Whom we are going. Each time we encounter new surprises, discoveries, and inspiration, the saying comes to mind: "The sign of God's work is when we are led where we did not plan to go."

For years, our church focused on serving the so-called poor, working with homeless people, youth groups, and in community development. Even with good results, however, we came to realize that having church and social ministry as two separate efforts resulted in a sort of spiritual schizophrenia. We were not living with those we wanted to serve. In fact, we were a bunch of well-intentioned, middle-class people crossing the city to do something we all believed was good.

After deeper reflection on the scriptures, we felt called to move our church from its original location in the Bom Retiro neighborhood of Curitiba, to Villa Fanny, a very poor neighborhood – not to only help them, but also to mend our own divided minds and actions. Still an institutional church, we adopted the motto: "We do not have a social ministry anymore; the church is the social ministry to the world." In Villa Fanny we found new work: we gardened, taught classical music, offered art classes, formed multilingual choirs, addressed environmental issues, started soap making, composted, and eventually transformed a parking lot into a garden with more than three hundred species – a place that teemed with life and the sounds of children.

Map by Cécile Marin, www.grida.no/graphicslib/detail/curitiba-location_88d1.

But we soon realized that our name "Casa" was nonsense: only a few of us actually lived in the area. We decided to move again, to where we could live our faith not just on Sundays but the whole week; not just in church, but in our homes and neighborhood, letting people see who we were with our families and activities. So we moved again, this time to Mossunguê, a more gentrified area, where we started Quinta da Videira ("Homestead of the Vine").

The urban farm we started here, in a tiny backyard of less than three hundred square yards, has led us further than any plan could have. Christian and secular organizations, universities, television programs, and research institutes have all come to see our simple garden and our daily life. It seems that the key to such an impact (even though our group of believers became smaller) grew clearer along the way: we were not launching a ministry or a project to serve people. Instead, we would just be there, with people, answering each challenge as best we could, trying to be honest, simple, and sincere while remaining biblically, scientifically, and technically serious about all our decisions and actions.

Starting with only a mustard seed, we began to see mountains start to move. We processed four tons of neighborhood garbage every month, produced four tons of food a year, shared common meals, received students from universities and colleges, wrote scientific articles on agriculture, and raised goats, chickens, and rabbits.

We called ourselves "urban farmers," not because it sounded trendy, but because that was the best way we found to express our loyalty to the God of creation. We have no loyalty to the false god called "market" and its mediator "money." Through gardening and composting, we create a new relationship with animals and plants: we are affirming another way of life, where the rhythms and balance of creation can express the freedom the Creator has promised us.

Naturally, this has not been well received by everyone. To some of our neighbors, we were spreading the fragrance of spiritual and technological knowledge; to others we smelled like horse manure. The city administration confronted us because of legal restrictions on farming in urban areas, but they ended up praising us as an example of environmental care for the city. Each barrier opened new doors and allowed the Lord to change our lives.

We did not have to advertise Jesus or our way of life with words; we had only to base our daily decisions on him. Once we honestly (and

The community offers young people training in "rural gardening."

Photographs courtesy of Claudio Oliver

Even the goats can share in community.

imperfectly) tried to follow the Lord, people who usually aren't interested in religion or in Jesus came by themselves. One example is a friend of mine, an atheist professor at the local university. Our reading of the scriptures and our care for creation affected him so much that now, whenever he brings his students to visit, he always says: "Show what you want . . . but please do not jump over your faith and why you do what you do."

Recently we moved again, this time to the rural area of Palmeira. Now, in partnership with a Mennonite group, we have started an "experimental station," surrounded by soy plantations, fracking, and tobacco farms. We hope to inspire small farmers with alternative and environmentally sound methods; we believe that a life based in scripture can lead to an abundance of life as opposed to the excesses of the market. So now, rather than calling ourselves urban farmers, we call ourselves rural gardeners. In this simple life we are called to love one another, and to build community.

As rural gardeners, our lack of mechanization and our attitude of care – both expressions of our faith – are starting to bear fruit. Small organic farmers are opening doors for us, calling us friends and wishing to know more about the scriptures and gardening.

We are not creating a model or a program, but we do hope to inspire other churches and groups to experiment more: that is, not to live under the obligation of "doing good," but to embrace contingency, caring for the neighbor you meet on the Jericho road, inspired by Jesus' example of love and readiness to serve. I know that the Lord will take you and your community to places and people you never dreamed of.

To learn more about Casa da Videira or watch an English-language video on their work, visit www.casadavideira.com.br.

From WikiArt (public domain)

Jean-François Millet, *The Man with the Hoe*

DANIEL J. STULAC

A Gospel of the Ground

Growing up, my siblings and I consumed generic canned vegetables and rehydrated milk while my father and mother scraped to put food on the table. I bear my parents no resentment for our culinary poverty. My father being a pastor, they did not have much money, and cheap food seemed a blessing at the time. In the 1980s, Wendell Berry's dictum that "eating is an agricultural act"[1] simply had not yet reached the dinner plates of Evangelical Presbyterians like us, and so we did not have a garden. I could not have said where squash or tomatoes come from, nor did I wonder. Food was fuel. The cheaper, the better.

Ten years after graduating college and a world away from my upbringing, I find myself in the little town of Piermont, New Hampshire, bracing a U-shaped calf-jack on the hindquarters of a Holstein named Wynette. The calf is in breech, and Lee is worried.[2] Two of its hooves stick out of the birth canal while its mother sways with exhaustion. She has been in labor all day, and would prefer to lie down. But for the well-being of her baby, Lee keeps her upright and attaches two chains to the calf's feet.

By this point in my life I have nearly a decade of agricultural experience under my belt. I have learned to cultivate beans, corn, apples, blueberries, broccoli, turnips, potatoes, peppers, and numerous other vegetables, fruits, and grains. But this summer is different. I am at Lee's farm on the banks of the Connecticut River to learn about the dairy business. My job is to hold the jack steady while Lee works the lever back and forth to winch the calf free. I am determined to perform well – a life, and a livelihood, hang in the balance. So does my pride.

Wynette feels the calf moving within her and begins to push. Without warning, a stream of manure shoots into the crisp June air. It seems to hang in space for a split second and then lands squarely on my forehead, spattering into my hair, my eyes and mouth, filling my ears and nose. I am spitting and coughing as it runs down my neck. The calf is moving; Lee is cheering. Braced firmly against the jack, eyes squeezed shut like a proselyte going under in the baptismal font, I refuse to abandon my

The author and his wife Sarah Messner served for two years in Rwinkwavu, Rwanda, as co-directors of agricultural development with Partners in Health (Rwanda). He is now a doctoral candidate in Old Testament studies at Duke University.

post. The stream becomes a river, and I am soon immersed.

A few minutes later, Lee drags the newborn animal across the barn floor and lifts it over a metal rail, face down, so that the amniotic fluid can drain from its nostrils and mouth – a real problem for breech birth calves, one that could easily lead to pneumonia and death if we are not careful. Wiping my glasses, I blink and try to get my bearings. Satisfied that both animals are now clear of immediate danger, Lee makes no effort to conceal his amusement at my condition. At church tomorrow he will have a rapturous tale to tell about the city slicker who thought he knew a little something about farming. "Well," he asks, grinning from ear to ear, "what will you name him?" I am conferred this honor since it is the first animal born under my care. "Carpaccio," I reply. "That was some raw beef."

We are creatures designed by God to get our hands dirty.

The gospel begins with a birth. Christians claim that the God of the universe has made a remarkable intrusion into the human predicament. The God of the Precambrian soup, the God of the Carboniferous forests, the God of the Cretaceous and the Pleistocene, the God of the triceratops and the wooly mammoth: that same God, Christians say, was born in a barn. What we do and how we live – everything about how we express the gospel in the world today – rests on these words from Philippians 2:

> Christ Jesus . . . being in very nature God, did not consider equality with God something to be grasped, but made himself nothing, taking the very nature of a servant, being made in human likeness . . . he humbled himself and became obedient to death – even death on a cross! (NIV 1984)

He made himself nothing, Paul says, *"taking the very nature of a servant."* How, we might ask, is Christ's servanthood related to his human likeness? What significance lies in the truth that the God of all creation loves creation so much that he enters into creation itself, that he participates in the raw, bodily, organic chemistry of it all?

American churches in particular have suffered protracted confusion on this issue. "Liberals" have tended to emphasize Christ's humanity over his divinity. The downside to such a scheme is that without the divinity of Christ, we are left without a savior, still needing something more than good advice from a good teacher who lived two thousand years ago. On the other hand, "conservatives" have tended to emphasize Christ's divinity at the expense of his humanity, as if Jesus were simply God "dressed up" in human flesh – not really human, but appearing human. This error fosters the ancient and pernicious idea that God's plan for salvation is to supply special, insider information to a select group of followers, who, through a little prayer and a little Gnostic magic, can be assured that God will snatch them from this world at just the right moment to spend eternity somewhere else. Destined to burn, the earth ceases to hold any real value. Like so many of our culture's labor-saving products, the earth becomes a disposable stage in the drama of Judgment Day. In this scheme, God is left without love.[3]

The Bible is clear: *God loved the world* in such a way that he gave to us his only Son (John 3:16). God loves the world with a passion that exceeds our own. God loves this planet and all its many inhabitants. When we fail to appreciate that God is human with us, that he made himself nothing and is the dust of the earth with us, the gospel comes to be more about psychology, more about feelings and fantasies, more about escaping, and less about God and God's deep and abiding love for his material creation.

A similar escapism manifests in the modern hope that humans will someday fly beyond our solar system to colonize other planets. Many believe that this is our destiny – to leave.[4] But a gospel rooted in incarnation – the human birth of God – has it the other way around. The gospel declares that God put us *here,* that God is *here,* and that God makes our home *here,* His home *here.* The gospel places us in the world that God loved in such a way that he gave his only Son on its behalf. In Christ, we do not escape our human bodies. Exactly the opposite! Rather than getting us out of our human skin, the gospel declares that God joins us. God joins us, down here amongst the malaria-ridden swamps and the dry, overworked hills. God makes our home his home. God declares this planet worth his time and attention.

That the Messiah should "take on the very nature of servant" is not an idea new to the New Testament. It derives primarily from Isaiah's Servant Songs, the most famous of which declares that the Servant will take up our infirmities and carry our sorrows (Isa. 53:4). Isaiah's Servant Songs envision the restoration of people to the land, and land to the people. Above all, they envision the restoration of God's intimate, immediate presence to a people exiled from their God and from their country. Christians see the completion, the fullness, of Isaiah's vision of restoration in Jesus. Thus, ultimate restoration in Christ is a restoration of *place.* God's incarnation – God's human birth – is a birth in the land, for the land, for those who live and subsist from the land (cf. Isa. 65:17–25; Rev. 22:1–5).

Tucked away in the middle of these Servant Songs lies an intriguing hint to Isaiah's redemptive vision. If we want to know what kind of restoration Isaiah has in view, if we want to know what kind of servant the Servant will be – what kind of work he will do, what kind of character he will have – then, the text suggests, we would do well to read the book of Genesis. Look to our parents, Abraham and Sarah, Isaiah advises us (51:2). Better yet, look to Eden. Read about the garden: "For the Lord will comfort Zion; he will comfort all her ruins. He will remake her desert like Eden, her wasteland like the garden of the Lord" (51:3).[5]

I suggest we take Isaiah at his word. If we want to know something about the Servant's mission on planet Earth, if we want to know what it means that God chooses human birth for himself, if we want to know what difference incarnation makes, if we want to know what

On the day the Lord God made the heavens and the earth – and no bush of the field had yet come to be in the earth, and no grass of the field had yet sprouted up, for the Lord God had not sent rain upon the earth, and there was no human *to serve the ground,* but a mist came up from the earth and watered the whole surface of the *ground* – the Lord God formed the human of *dust from the ground,* and he breathed into his nostrils the breath of life, and the human became a living soul. And the Lord God planted a garden, in Eden, in the east, and there he put the human whom he had formed.

And the Lord God took the human and he *placed* him in the garden of Eden *to serve it and to keep it.* (Gen. 2:4–8, 15; author's translation).

Henri Rousseau, detail from *Exotic Landscape*

From WikiArt (public domain)

Christ restores and redeems through the cross and resurrection, Isaiah says: Look back at the beginning. Look back to the garden in which humanity was created.

According to Genesis 2, we are the dust of the earth. The word for "human being" in Hebrew, *ʾādām,* or the name Adam as the first human is called, derives from the same root as does the word for "ground" or "soil," which is *ʾadāmāh*. In other words, human beings are "groundlings." Every cell in our bodies is made of organic molecules – carbon, oxygen, hydrogen – atoms which were, at one time or another, floating through the atmosphere of our planet, falling down through the clouds as rain, percolating through the soil, being absorbed into the roots of plants, dying and decomposing and living again in the bodies of new plants and new animals.

The gospel of Jesus Christ is good news born in a barn.

We are, quite literally, born of dust. But that does not mean we are only dust. Filled with the breath of God, we have a special vocation, too – to serve the garden in which God placed us, and to keep it well. As dust of the earth, we are created to be servants of the soil. We are creatures designed by God to have our hands dirty. We are intended for cultivation. We are here as the keepers, the pruners, the grafters, the midwives, and the husbands of God's planet. We are of creation, and we are for creation. And as creatures, we are part of creation. It is precisely here, in our raw creatureliness as described in Genesis, in our abject organismal state, that God chooses to abide with us. God – the God who made the dust, who made the stars, who made the elements of which we are composed – that same God chooses from the beginning to make his dwelling among us, to live for all time like us, as a servant of the soil. I am the dust of the earth, but God declares that he is not too good, not too proud, for my dustiness.

Lee has beaten me to church. I can already hear him cackling in the sanctuary. The whole congregation of fifty will know my story, told and retold, before the morning is over. It is all in good fun, and I will play my part in Lee's rapidly evolving melodrama.

But for the time being, I am standing in the foyer just outside, transfixed. Hanging above me is a life-size painting of Jesus striding through the grass with a lamb in his arms. I have walked past this picture perhaps fifty or sixty times already this summer. Historically speaking, suggests my seminary education, the portrait is quite misguided, quite wrong. For Jesus, as we all know, did not have blue eyes. He did not have rolling locks of sandy brown hair, pale skin, or a long, European nose. In no place do the Gospels suggest that Jesus worked directly with animals or performed any farm labor whatsoever. In many (especially urban) communities, this portrait would come across as saccharine at best, racially offensive at worst. But why, I wonder, have I been willing to account for only its "errors"? Is such a representation of Jesus really as "wrong" as I have assumed? On the morning after Carpaccio came feet-first into this world, I am having second thoughts.

Piermont, New Hampshire, is a small community with a deep history in the land. A blinking, yellow light hangs from a wire in the center of town. The corner store and gas station sells cigarettes, beer, hardware, and scooped ice cream in season. An inn, salon, and post office can be found around the corner. Moose and bear are not rare sights, even close to the center of town.

Jean-François Millet, *Peasants Bringing Home a Calf Born in the Fields*

From WikiArt (public domain)

When Lee and his wife Betty Sue married in 1970, Piermont boasted twenty-five farms. Dairy was the economic backbone of the community. Since then, however, selling milk to Cabot, the regional dairy cooperative, has ceased to make economic sense. Family farmers took on mortgages, hoping the downward trend would prove only temporary. At one point Lee and Betty Sue were selling their milk for half of what it cost to produce. They have survived only because their son Mark is an exceptional cheese maker, turning their high quality milk into an artisanal product that is to be sold to restaurants as far away as Boston and New York. Lee and Betty Sue are the exception. If Mark's son Eli someday farms their quiet bend in the Connecticut River, he will become a seventh generation dairyman, truly defying the economic odds that Big Dairy has stacked against him.[6] A few weeks after Carpaccio's birthday, the number of farms in Piermont would drop even lower as yet another family, two miles down the road, cashed out and sold their herd. Now Lee and Betty Sue are one of just five farms left.

Looking deeply into Jesus' blue eyes, I am struck that in a rural community historically devoted to animal husbandry, this little country church decided to hang in its front foyer a portrait of Christ the Good Shepherd. Not Christ in prayer, not Christ the teacher, not Christ the miracle-worker. Not even Christ on the cross, although all of these images would have been "accurate." No, Piermont Congregational Church chose to characterize its faith through a portrait of Christ the farmer. Christ, whose arms are wrapped around a sheep. Christ, who knows late nights in the barn and early mornings in the pasture. Christ, who knows the backbreaking work of hay season. Christ, who knows the gut-wrenching worry of a failed harvest. Christ of the newborn lamb. Christ of the breeched calf. Christ of the miscarriage. Christ of the compost pile. Christ of the filthy fingernails.

Jesus, being in very nature God, did not consider equality with God something to be grasped, but made himself nothing, taking the very nature of a servant (Phil. 2:6–7) – being born of worldly dust. A truly Trinitarian gospel implies that our humanity, our "dustiness," is not a problem for God. Human birth is not God's emergency Plan B for the world. On the contrary, our creatureliness is precisely what God loves about us. It is precisely what he redeems and restores.

The gospel of Jesus Christ is *not* a gospel of escape, a nugget of insider information that gets the believer off the hook while the world burns in the rearview mirror. The gospel of Jesus Christ is a gospel of emplacement. It is good news born in a barn. It is a gospel of the ground.

1. Wendell Berry, "The Pleasures of Eating," in *The Art of the Commonplace: The Agrarian Essays of Wendell Berry,* ed. Norman Wirzba (Counterpoint, 2002), 321.
2. Personal names and descriptions are used with permission.
3. Norman Wirzba, "Placing the Soul: An Agrarian Philosophical Principle," in *The Essential Agrarian Reader: The Future of Culture, Community, and the Land,* ed. Norman Wirzba (University Press of Kentucky, 2003), 80–86.
4. Ellen F. Davis, *Scripture, Culture, and Agriculture: An Agrarian Reading of the Bible* (Cambridge University Press, 2009), 81. Davis cites Carl Sagan, *Pale Blue Dot: A Vision of the Human Future in Space* (Random House, 1994), 385.
5. All Old Testament translations and emphases are the author's.
6. For a comprehensive analysis of the history of dairy farming in New England, see Kirk Kardashian, *Milk Money: Cash, Cows, and the Death of the American Dairy Farm* (University of New Hampshire Press, 2012).

Sacred Seeds

MARY EUBANKS

How Ancient Genes Can Help End Hunger, Save the Soil, and Equip Small Farmers to Face Climate Change

From *imgkid.com* (public domain)

The maize plants growing in my experimental greenhouse were starting to flower. When I started shaking the pollen from the tassels onto the silks of individual plants, a task I'd done countless times during my years as a maize genetics researcher, something strange happened. First, I started having trouble breathing. Soon I was gasping for air and my body started swelling up; before long my eyes were swollen shut. The alarmed greenhouse manager rushed me to the emergency room. I was experiencing anaphylactic shock, an extreme allergic reaction that can be fatal without immediate treatment. As I began to recover, I broke out in a blistery rash. It took a round of strong steroids and a month before I fully recuperated.

My doctors were concerned that I had become sensitive to maize pollen, which would mean my career in maize genetics was over. When I explained to them that the maize I was pollinating was one I'd never worked with before – a new genetically engineered (GM) variety – they began to suspect the cause of my reaction. Could it be that the foreign substances in GM pollen were triggering my immune system? Tests eventually bore out their hunch.

This dramatic first brush with GM maize,

Mary Eubanks is an adjunct professor of biology at Duke University and founder and president of Sun Dance Genetics, a company that is developing drought- and disease-resistant corn varieties. In collaboration with African partners, she works to make seeds from these new varieties available to small farmers in South Sudan and West Africa.

which had then recently been approved for commercial sale in the United States, was almost twenty years ago. Last year, a peer-reviewed study confirmed that such allergic responses can be caused by inhalation of GM pollen.[1] In the meantime, though, my own work had taken a surprising turn – one that seems to hold the promise of an alternative to the genetic engineering not only of maize but of other major food crops as well.

A Poisoned Promise

Our ancient ancestors lived close to the earth and were keenly aware of how vulnerable their food supply was to the forces of nature. The seeds that provided their food were sacred. Grains such as maize and wheat were viewed as gifts from the gods and revered as the source of life.

A K'iche' Maya burial urn depicting the maize god

Today, by contrast, most of our food is grown on large-scale industrialized farms using heavy machinery, patented seeds, and intensive use of synthetic fertilizers and pesticides. In spite of growing consumer concern, most people remain unaware of how their food is produced or the harm that industrialized farming is causing the environment and human health.

Almost all corn, soy, cotton, canola, and sugar beets grown in the United States and Canada are genetically engineered. Such crops are known as genetically modified organisms (GMOs). Since they provide important ingredients in the production of processed foods, approximately 80 percent of all food products on grocery shelves in the United States today contain GMOs.

In order to create a GMO, researchers alter a plant by inserting a foreign gene – either a gene from another species such as a bacterium, virus, animal, or other plant, or a synthesized gene that has never occurred in nature. Researchers hitch this gene to a reporter gene so that it can enter the host plant and cause it to express the desired traits.

Most GM crops are engineered for insect resistance and herbicide tolerance (HT). Initially, HT crops were widely welcomed, because they ushered in an era of no-till agriculture. When the HT seed emerges, the field is sprayed with its associated herbicide – most often glyphosate, manufactured by Monsanto under the name RoundUp – which kills the weeds without injuring the crop. Since this procedure eliminates tilling for weed control, it promised to reduce soil erosion, carbon emissions, fuel and machinery costs, and farmers' time and effort.

In the early years, GM crops seemed to make good on that promise: herbicide use in the United States declined. But weeds soon began to evolve resistance to the herbicides,[2] so that between 2001 and 2007 the amount of herbicide applied in the United States increased by one hundred million pounds. In parts of the country, in fact, weeds have become an even more serious problem for farmers than they were before HT crops were introduced. The industry's response has been to engineer crops that will tolerate stronger, more toxic herbicides like 2,4-D, the active ingredient in Agent Orange.

A similar story has played out with crops engineered for insect resistance. To combat insect pests, researchers used the Bt gene from *Bacillus thuringiensis,* a soil bacterium; this gene acts as a plant-incorporated insecticide. Initially, Bt crops allowed farmers to spray less chemicals. But insects also rapidly evolved resistance, and farmers are now applying more insecticides to protect GMO crops than previously.[3] The unintended victims have included

Photograph by Justin Kerr

Monarch butterflies, whose numbers have dropped precipitously in recent years.

Such ill effects don't seem to be outliers. Mounting evidence suggests that GM-based agriculture has decreased soil fertility, caused soil acidification through salt build-up from heavy chemical use, increased pollution of water supplies from agricultural run-off, and destroyed beneficial insects and soil microbes at an alarming rate. While there is no scientific consensus on GMO safety,[4] a number of studies have raised concerns about risks to human health.[5] The mantra of the biotechnology industry is that genetically engineered crops are necessary to produce enough food to feed the world's burgeoning population. However, data comparing yields of GM crops to non-GM crops do not support this argument.[6] Nor do claims that it is faster to develop new varieties using genetic engineering hold up under scrutiny.[7]

In light of the harm caused by industrial agriculture and GMO technology, the United Nations has called for "a paradigm shift in agricultural development: from a 'green revolution' to an 'ecological intensification' approach."[8] To many, such language may sound impractical and unrealistic. My research, however, suggests there are good grounds not to resign ourselves too easily to the current state of farming.

A Botanical Mystery

Agriculture first emerged around ten thousand years ago when humans began cultivating plants and living in village settlements. This shift from hunting and gathering occurred as big game was dying out when the climate warmed at the end of the last Ice Age. With climate change, species migrated into new ecological niches, bringing them into proximity with related species. This led to cross-pollinations that gave rise to hybrids with novel characteristics such as larger seeds and fruits, less shattering so seeds remained on plants during harvest, uniform ripening, and loss of hard seed coats and thorns. Modern crops originated from human selection of the genetic variation in these naturally occurring hybrids.

Against this background, the origin of maize in particular has been one of the great botanical mysteries. The large edible ears of maize that we enjoy today – firm cobs each holding hundreds of kernels – are in fact an ancient human invention, and maize would quickly go extinct if humans did not plant, harvest, and preserve it. Yet maize does not look at all like either of its two wild relatives, teosinte and gamagrass. How did this remarkable plant arise in the first place?

That's the question with which I began my career as an anthropologist specializing in American archaeology; my PhD research was on ancient maize. In the late 1970s, a new teosinte was discovered in the mountains of Jalisco, Mexico. This plant, perennial and more primitive than other teosinte species, sparked a new theory and new experimental research on maize's origins.

As an archaeologist, I knew if I was to ever understand the maize story I needed to learn

Caves in the Tlacolula valley in Oaxaca, Mexico, where the earliest evidence of domesticated teosinte, an ancestor of maize, was found. Teosinte kernels found in one cave, Guilá Naquitz, date to before 5400 BC.

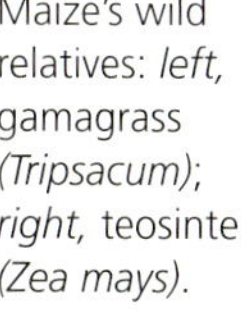

Maize's wild relatives: *left,* gamagrass *(Tripsacum)*; *right,* teosinte *(Zea mays)*.

Photographs from Wikimedia commons, (public domain)

more about genetics. I began assisting Paul C. Mangelsdorf, a botanist famous for his theory on the origin of maize, in his new research into the origin of annual teosintes. In the process, we mapped the gene in maize coding for perennialism, the trait allowing the plant to live for two years or more.[9] This unprecedented discovery opened up a new line of research – imagine a yet-to-be-developed maize variety that didn't need to be seeded every year, but just kept coming up every spring like many wild grasses do. I left my university job teaching anthropology to become a postdoctoral fellow in maize genetics.

Hybrid Power

In my experimental research, I made the first successful crosses between teosinte and gamagrass. The result was fertile plants that produced tiny ears resembling the oldest archaeological maize remains found in dry caves in southern Mexico.[10] Since the scientific name for Eastern gamagrass is *Tripsacum dactyloides,* we dubbed the resulting hybrids Tripsacorn. This discovery has profound implications for maize improvement because these hybrids are cross-fertile with maize.

Cross-fertility matters because the Tripsacorn provides a genetic bridge that breaks the sterility barrier between maize and gamagrass. Wild relatives like gamagrass are a rich reservoir of genes that enable survival under harsh conditions, so tapping their genetic diversity has traditionally been an important tool in plant breeding. In the case of maize, the rich genetic diversity of gamagrass can now be tapped to breed new strains of maize with traits for drought and heat tolerance, resistance to insects and disease, high protein, and enhanced nitrogen efficiency, reducing the need for fertilizer. In other words, this discovery opened up the possibility for sustainable maize farming.

The first proof of concept came when I selected lines that had native resistance to corn rootworm, one of the billion-dollar bugs of maize.[11] Corn rootworm refers to beetle larvae that hatch in the soil at the time maize seedlings are sprouting and feed on their roots. Growers can lose as much as half their crop to corn rootworm damage. Accordingly, insecticides used to control corn rootworm are some of the most toxic in the world. While there is a GM variety of maize with a plant-incorporated insecticide, the insect has rapidly evolved resistance to it.

Because gamagrass is native to the plains of North America, where it co-evolved with corn rootworm, it naturally tolerates this expensive pest. In my breeding program, I selected gamagrass-introgressed maize lines with strong rootworm tolerance. Native tolerance, rather than poisoning the insects, derives its effect from air passages present in the roots, a characteristic of gamagrass. Thus, in contrast with the solid roots of maize, roots of native-trait maize do not provide adequate nutrition for the corn rootworm larvae to thrive. An added benefit of this mechanism is that the air passages enable the roots to penetrate deep into the soil below the hardpan, where they can access water. In fact, feeding by the larvae stimulates root growth, and the larger root systems boost yield and help protect against drought. In addition, the air passages attract

Below left: Is this what the earliest maize looked like? Ears of gammagrass, *left,* teosinte, *right,* and the gammagrass–teosinte hybrid, *center,* developed by the author.

Below right: Root systems of Tripsacorn, *left,* and commercial Bt maize, *right.* Deeper roots provide drought resistance and greater vigor in poor soils.

Photographs courtesy of Mary Eubanks

nitrogen-fixing bacteria to the roots, reducing the need for synthetic fertilizer.

All in all, that is a fairly impressive list of beneficial traits. It's also a revealing illustration of how we can tap ancestral genes to adapt our modern crops for ecologically sustainable agriculture. Tripsacorn maize does not destroy the insect that provides food for birds. It does not require chemical additives that kill beneficial soil organisms and cause soil acidification and compaction. Instead, it helps build up soil fertility by attracting nitrogen-fixing bacteria and improves soil permeability by naturally tilling the soil with its deep roots.

In order to test whether the native-trait lines were as good as we hoped, we conducted multi-year field trials comparing rootworm efficacy for Tripsacorn maize and Bt maize. The Bt maize had lower scores for larval feeding on the roots than the new maize; meanwhile, the new maize had bigger root systems and higher grain yields than the Bt maize. Since corn is a multibillion dollar industry, we felt these findings were of more than just academic interest.

We submitted our results to a scientific journal for publication. The editor showed the manuscript to Monsanto, the only company at the time that had GM maize seed on the market; in response, the company threatened to sue the journal if it accepted the paper. In the end, our study was published only after we expunged the results for Bt maize. Our experience doesn't seem to be an isolated episode; other scientists trying to conduct independent research on GM crops have reported similar treatment.[12]

Such strong-arm techniques only mask a growing problem in American agriculture. In the United States, as acreage planted in GMO crops has increased to more than 90 percent, there has been a huge shift in resources and funding into biotechnology and away from plant breeding.[13] A few companies still sell non-GM seed, but it is getting harder for farmers to find. When the price of maize dropped in 2014 to pre-biotechnology prices, however, many farmers began re-thinking the economics of planting GM crops, and seed companies are scrambling to meet a sudden demand for non-GM seed.[14]

Several US companies have made offers to license my genetic-bridge technology with the stipulation that they be allowed to convert it to GM maize. Since I want my discovery to help reduce the use of harmful chemicals, I've turned them down. (Tripsacorn maize is under development for the commercial market in Europe, where most countries do not plant GM maize.)

New Maize in Africa

For the foreseeable future, then, plant breeding using ancestral genes will continue to face resistance in developed countries dominated by the biotechnology-chemical treadmill. Thankfully, however, a far larger group of farmers stands to benefit much more quickly: subsistence growers in developing countries, who lack the resources and infrastructure for industrial agriculture.

In much of the world, basic crops like maize have a life-and-death importance that Westerners often fail to recognize. Although industrialized countries use maize mainly for livestock feed or as a raw material for manufactured products, it is the staple food for half the population of sub-Saharan Africa. Higher yielding than any other grain, maize is easy to digest and serves as a crucial source of carbohydrates, protein, iron, vitamin B, and

Children pitch in at the first Tripsacorn harvest in South Sudan.

minerals. It is consumed in a wide variety of forms: fresh, dried, roasted; ground and eaten in porridges, grits, and pastes; and brewed into beer. It can be stored for long periods of time and thus fills the hunger gap during the long dry season. Every part of the plant can be used to produce a variety of food and non-food products.

This South Sudanese school depends on produce from the school garden to help feed the children.

I made the first crosses between gamagrass and teosinte in 1984, a year with a devastating drought in Ethiopia. The pictures of starving children broke my heart, and I prayed that one day my research might help relieve hunger in Africa. In 1998, a student brought me seeds of a traditional African open-pollinated maize variety he purchased in a Ghana market. I grew the tropical maize, cross-pollinated it with Tripsacorn lines, and saved the seed.

Below, Ears of Tripsacorn hang outside Renk Theological College, South Sudan.

Ten years later I met Daniel Deng Bul Yak, now the archbishop of the Episcopal Church of Sudan and South Sudan. When I described this maize to him, he wanted to try growing it, and I gave him seed to take back to Sudan. It was planted in the garden of Renk Theological College in Upper Nile State, an area where the rich soil was stripped bare of all vegetation in the bitter fighting that raged in that highly contested region. Today, this maize is providing food for students in South Sudan, while seeds are being saved from each crop cycle and plans are underway to increase production to help feed refugees returning from the north and Ethiopia.

As one of Africa's most hunger-threatened nations, South Sudan is precisely the kind of country in which ancestral-gene breeding can make the biggest impact. Millions were killed and displaced here during five decades of civil war, and the basic skills of survival in an agrarian economy were lost to a generation that grew up in refugee camps. Now that many have come home, the four-year-old Republic of South Sudan faces a massive challenge feeding its people. War ravaged the cattle herds and crops in countless villages, destroying seed and root stocks along with markets and other forms of traditional infrastructure. Chronic malnutrition is widespread.

Here the high protein content of Tripsacorn maize can be lifesaving: at 17.4 percent, it is more than double that of either sorghum (7.9 percent) or standard maize (7.8 percent). This variety also has elevated levels of essential amino acids that the body needs to build proteins it cannot produce itself.

Apart from war, another threat to food security in South Sudan and East Africa is postharvest loss of grain: weevils consume as much as 25 percent of maize stored for the dry season. Experiments conducted by James Throne, a USDA entomologist, demonstrated that several lines of Tripsacorn maize have a staggering 100 percent native resistance to grain weevil.[15] This could be decisive for smallholder farm families whose maize is stored for months outdoors in granaries made from natural materials, or hanging from the ceilings of their homes. Other traits that can be particularly beneficial for South Sudan include resistance to insects, disease, and the African parasitic weed *Striga,* as well as enhanced nitrogen efficiency, enabling plant growth in poor soils.

Photographs courtesy of Mary Eubanks

The first planting of Tripsacorn maize outside a school in Unity State, South Sudan

Ancient Genes and Climate Change

Apart from poverty and war, South Sudan faces another threat, one it shares with many developing countries: global warming. Climate-change models predict increased heat and drought for much of South Sudan. Fortunately, Tripsacorn maize stands out for its very high level of drought and heat tolerance.

I had seen indications of this property of the new maize in early field observation and growth-chamber experiments. But it was not until 2011, while on sabbatical in Texas during the worst drought on record there, that I discovered just how exceptional Tripsacorn really is. I had planted a small dry-land plot at the University of Texas in Austin. Already at planting time there was a twenty-seven-inch deficit in rainfall. In the weeks that followed, no rain came. I had not installed an irrigation system, though I occasionally hand-watered when the plants appeared stressed. By early June, all the commercial-variety control plants were dead. Yet the Tripsacorn plants remained green and were producing ears. I looked forward to being able to report glowing results. Then one night raccoons came in and destroyed the entire crop, and I abandoned the plot.

When I returned in late July, at the far back of the plot I found, much to my surprise, some green maize plants. Even more surprising, they were producing silks and pollen under conditions of extreme heat and moisture deficit: the average high temperature since planting had been 37.1 degrees Celsius (98.8 degrees Fahrenheit). Although maize pollen and silks are not viable above 32 degrees Celsius, I pollinated these exceptional ears anyway. I watered them on the day of pollination, and again one week later. The temperature ranged from 39 to 40.6 degrees Celsius the days I pollinated, and the average high temperature of 40 degrees Celsius (104 degrees Fahrenheit) continued throughout the month of August. No rain fell in July or August. Even so, the maize plants bore seed, and three of the ears were completely filled out. Such extreme drought and heat tolerance in maize is unprecedented.

I realized a seed like this could be game-changing for the millions of subsistence farmers most threatened by climate change. The following year, I worked with Nyuol Tong, a South Sudanese student at Duke University who had founded a school in his home village to help educate his people. We made crosses of gamagrass-introgressed African maize with the exceptionally drought- and heat-tolerant maize discovered during the Texas drought. In 2013 Mr. Tong took seed of several varieties we created to his home in upper Unity State, South Sudan, and it was planted in the school garden.

In this part of Africa, a school garden is no

mere side project. If the school can provide a meal, children will come; for many children it may be the only food they have to eat for the day. To our joy, the first planting of the maize grew well and yielded a bountiful harvest.

Looking to the future, our goal is to select varieties well adapted to the region's growing conditions and local food preferences. Any surplus seed left after feeding the children will be distributed to neighboring farmers and sold at market. This will generate income for the school and food security for the whole community. A long-term goal is to launch a participatory breeding program, in which the farmers learn how to grow higher yielding, locally adapted hybrid maize. The new hybrid maize could be the basis for forming an indigenous start-up seed company. In 2015, we will begin testing Tripsacorn maize in a new project in West Africa.

Working with Nature

What wider lessons can we learn from the success of ancestral-gene breeding in maize? It's time to take an anthropological approach to agriculture, one that takes its clues from antiquity and from traditional farming practices and is oriented to the needs and preferences of local communities. By blending innovative modern science with indigenous knowledge, we can significantly enhance the food security, nutrition, and health of resource-poor farmers without undermining their cultural heritage or damaging the environment.

Improving crops through hybridization with wild relatives is a time-honored tradition in plant breeding. The model presented here is a promising alternative to the increasing use of GMOs and agrichemicals in Africa and elsewhere. It's an approach that works *with* nature, introducing traits that evolved naturally and thus do not lose efficacy over time. This is one way we can fulfill the United Nations' mandate to move away from the "green revolution" based on genetically modified seeds and heavy use of fertilizers and pesticides to an approach that is sustainable and regenerative, enabling farmers to be good stewards of the earth.

1. M. Andreassen, E. Rocca, O.G. Wikmark, J. Van der Berg, T. Traavik, "Humoral and cellular immune response in mice after airway administration of Bacillus thuriengensis Cry1Ab and MON810 cry1Ab-transgenic maize," *Food and Agricultural Immunology* (2014).
2. Major M. Goodman, James B. Holland, and Jesus Sánchez G., "Breeding and Genetic Diversity," in *Genetics, Genomics and Breeding of Maize,* ed. Ramakrishna Wusirika, Martin Bohn, Jinsheng Lai, Chittaranjan Kole (Boca Raton, FL: CRC Press, 2014), 14–50.
3. Aaron J. Gassman, Jennifer L. Petzold-Maxwell, Ryan S. Keweshan, Mike W. Dunbar, "Field-evolved Resistance to Bt Maize by Western Corn Rootworm," *PLOS ONE* 6, no. 7, (2011).
4. European Network of Scientists for Social and Environmental Responsibility, "No Scientific Consensus on GMO Safety," ENSSER Statement, 21 October 2013.
5. Mary Eubanks, "Allergies á la Carte: Is There a Problem with Genetically Modified Foods?" *Environmental Health Perspectives* (March 2002): A130.
6. Jorge Fernandez-Cornejo, Seth Wechsler, Mike Livingston, and Lorraine Mitchell, "Genetically Engineered Crops in the United States," *ERR Report 162,* United States Department of Agriculture Economic Research Service (2014): 12.
7. Major M. Goodman, "New Sources of Germplasm: Lines, Transgenes, and Breeders," in *Memoria Congresso Nacional de Fitogenetica,* ed. J.M. Martinez, F. Rincon S., and G. Martinez G. (Saltillo, Mexico: Univ. Autonino Agr. Antonio Narro, 2002), 28–41.
8. United Nations Conference on Trade and Development, "Wake Up Before It's Too Late: Make Agriculture Truly Sustainable Now for Food Security in a Changing Climate," UNCTAD Trade and Environment Review 2013.
9. Paul C. Mangelsdorf and Mary Eubanks Dunn, "Linkage relations of Pe*-d," *Maize Genetics Cooperation Newsletter* 58: 53.
10. Mary Eubanks,"A Genetic Bridge to Utilize Tripsacum Germplasm in Maize Improvement," *Maydica* 51 (2006): 315.
11. D. Prischmann, M. Eubanks, K. Dashiel, D. Schneider, "Evaluating Tripsacum-introgressed Maize Germplasm After Infestation with Western Corn Rootworm (Coleoptera: Chrysomelidae)," *Journal of Economic Entomology* 133 (2009): 10.
12. Emily Waltz, "Under Wraps," *Nature Biotechnology* 27, no. 10, (October 2009): 880. See also Emily Waltz, "Battlefield," *Nature* 461, (3 September 2009): 27.
13. Bill Tracey and Michael Sligh (eds.), *Proceedings of the 2014 Summit on Seeds and Breeds for 21st Century Agriculture* (Pittsboro, North Carolina: Rural Advancement Foundation International, RAFI-USA, 2014).
14. Jacob Bunge, "Fields of Gold: GMO-Free Crops Prove Lucrative for Farmers," *Wall Street Journal,* February 2, 2015.
15. James E. Throne and Mary Eubanks, "Resistance of Tripsacorn to Storage Insect Pests," *Journal of Stored Products Research* 28 (2002): 239.

Firewood

The bent oak by the tool shed is dying.
Now in late April, you can clearly see
the deadened wood at each extremity
encircled by the bright first leaves of spring.

One day soon my saw will bite
into the base of that tough old trunk;
careful notch cut out the front,
back cut, wedge, and then timber.
Give or take 100 years
of life and growth come crashing right

between two cherry ornamentals;
chainsaw precision.
The air a rich infusion:
burning oil and petrol smoke,
tangy sour of fresh cut oak,
crushed wild garlic and bluebells.

In this moment though, the late sun halos
the soft bright green against the bark's brown grey,
The slightest of breezes whispering by,
it seems the chorus of rooks crescendos.

Ian Barth

Photograph by Theophilos Papadopoulos

Marianne North, *Trees Laden with Parasites and Epiphytes in a Brazilian Garden*

From WikiArt (public domain)

Insights

Barbara Kingsolver I was trained as a biologist, and I can appreciate the challenge and the technical mastery involved in isolating, understanding, and manipulating genes. . . . But I only have to stand still for a minute and watch the outcome of thirty million years' worth of hummingbird evolution transubstantiated before my eyes into nest and egg to get knocked down to size. I have held in my hand the germ of a plant engineered to grow, yield its crop, and then murder its own embryos, and there I glimpsed the malevolence that can lie in the heart of a profiteering enterprise. There once was a time when Thoreau wrote, "I have great faith in a seed. Convince me that you have a seed there, and I am prepared to expect wonders." By the power vested in everything living, let us keep to that faith. I'm a scientist who thinks it wise to enter the doors of creation not with a lion tamer's whip and chair, but with the reverence humankind has traditionally summoned for entering places of worship: a temple, a mosque, or a cathedral. A sacred grove, as ancient as time.

Pope John Paul II Faced with the glory of the Trinity in creation, we must contemplate, sing, and rediscover awe. . . . But this capacity for contemplation and knowledge, this discovery of a transcendent presence in creation, must also lead us to rediscover our fraternity with the earth, to which we have been linked since creation. This very goal was foreshadowed by the Old Testament in the Hebrew Jubilee, when the earth rested and man gathered what the land spontaneously offered (Lev. 25:11–12). If nature is not violated and humiliated, it returns to being the sister of humanity.

Flannery O'Connor Where you have absolute solutions, you have no need of faith. Faith is what you have in the absence of knowledge. The reason this clash doesn't bother me any longer is because I have got, over the years, a sense of the immense sweep of creation, of the evolutionary process in everything, of how incomprehensible God must necessarily be to be the God of heaven and earth. You can't fit the Almighty into your intellectual categories.

Wendell Berry The Bible leaves no doubt at all about the sanctity of the act of world-making, or of the world that was made, or of creaturely or bodily life in this world. We are holy creatures living among other holy creatures in a world that is holy. Some people know this, and some do not. Nobody, of course, knows it all the time. But what keeps it from being far better known than it is? Why is it apparently unknown to millions of professed students of the Bible? How can modern Christianity have so solemnly folded its hands while so much of the work of God was and is being destroyed?

Barbara Kingsolver, *Small Wonder* (Harper Collins, 2002), 108. Pope John Paul II, general audience, January 26, 2000, Zenit translation. Flannery O'Connor, *The Habit of Being* (Farrar, Straus and Giroux, 1979), 476–477. Wendell Berry, *The Art of the Commonplace*, ed. Norman Wirzba (Counterpoint, 2002), 309.

JOHN MURDOCK

Conservation Is for Conservatives

Rescuing Creation from the Fog of the Culture War

"What has brought about the ugly destruction of the environment? There is one reason: man's greed." Today some evangelical power brokers might roll their eyes at such a statement, dismissing it as the hyperbolic ramblings of a tree-hugging leftist. If told that this came from a Christian, they might doubt the person's faith, or warn of what liberal positions would follow now that the person has been "blinded by the green light and lost his sense of direction," as the Family Research Council's Tony Perkins once put it.

Piet Mondrian, *Village Church*

From WikiArt (public domain)

Those opening words, though, were penned by Francis Schaeffer – a pastor who read the Bible through a literalist lens but who with his wife Edith extended hospitality to all sorts at their L'Abri home in the Swiss Alps. Schaeffer, a best-selling author, reshaped the trajectory of evangelical cultural engagement and inspired right-wing culture warriors from the Reverend Jerry Falwell to Congresswoman Michele Bachmann. Schaeffer's plea for creation was followed not by an embrace of the left's sexual permissiveness but by a call to elevate evangelical concern for the unborn.

Abortion went on to become the primary "glue which holds religiosity and partisanship together," according to Robert Putnam and David Campbell's book *American Grace,* an influential exploration into religion and civic life. Environmentalism, meanwhile, became bonded to liberalism despite having diverse and deep roots that extend across the philosophical spectrum.

Russell Kirk, whose *The Conservative Mind* remains a classic text of the modern right, once said: "The issue of environmental quality is one which transcends traditional political boundaries. It is a cause which can attract, and very sincerely, liberals, conservatives, radicals, reactionaries, freaks, and middle class straights." While some conservatives such as Roger Scruton, author of *How to Think Seriously about the Planet: The Case for Environmental Conservatism,* still demonstrate the truth of Kirk's sentiment, a squeamishness about being seen with liberals has led most to abandon the field. What's more, many now feel it is their duty to disparage those conservatives who stayed behind.

Political tribalism split apart concerns that, as Schaeffer demonstrated, can be held consistently and passionately within a biblical

John Murdock, a self-styled "Christian conservative tree-hugger," worked as a natural-resources attorney in Washington, DC for over a decade and now writes from a family farmhouse deep in the heart of his native Texas. www.johnmurdock.org

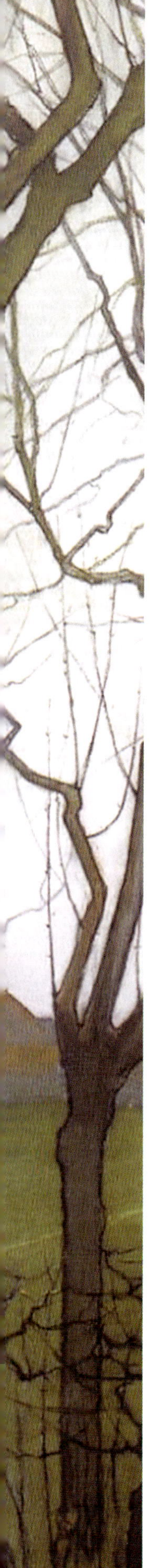

worldview. Schaeffer wrote of once going out of his way to compliment the residents of a lushly landscaped hippie commune which stood on the other side of a deep valley from a treeless Christian school campus he was visiting. Those who warmly greeted him noted that he was the first to come from "across the ravine." In the decades since, the chasm between socially conservative evangelicals and planet-conserving environmentalists has only grown wider.

That Seventies Show

The current political blocs that have greens and gays on one side and pro-lifers chanting "drill baby drill" on the other can seem set in stone, but the cement was wet and malleable as recently as the 1970s. Evangelicals for McGovern existed well before the Moral Majority. Richard Nixon created the Environmental Protection Agency and enthusiastically signed major bipartisan bills such as the Clean Air Act and the Endangered Species Act, the latter sailing through the House on a 355–4 vote. *Roe v. Wade* was initially deemed a proper balance of church–state relations by prominent Southern Baptists. A favorite politician for both Jim Wallis and Billy Graham was Senator Mark Hatfield of Oregon, a pro-life, antiwar, liberal, evangelical, often environmentalist Republican. Two Earth Days competed on the calendar: a spring-equinox date that was championed by a pro-life Pentecostal pacifist named John McConnell, and a larger April celebration linked to the liberal Democratic Senator Gaylord Nelson. Pat Robertson, who would seek the Republican presidential nomination in 1988, backed Jimmy Carter's presidential bid in 1976.

One does wonder how things might have turned out if Carter, the former Navy man at the helm of the Democratic ship when the abortion storm arose in earnest, had steered a different course. Up till then, abortion had not yet cracked party platforms, but in 1972, traditionally Democratic Catholics had beaten back a pro-choice platform proposal and gained a pro-lifer on the ticket in Sargent Shriver. These voters were stunned when their party's 1976 platform came out explicitly opposing a human-life amendment.

Though he would later identify as pro-choice, the politically pragmatic President Ford saw an opening. His prospective Republican running mate Bob Dole consulted with the campaign of Democratic presidential candidate Ellen McCormack, a New York pro-life activist who had garnered up to nine percent of the vote in several primaries. The GOP followed McCormack's advice and went on record as officially supporting a constitutional "right to life for unborn children." Nevertheless, the Democrats' openly "born again" Sunday school teacher was still able to garner significant evangelical support and nip Ford overall.

President Carter thought his personal piety would be enough to keep evangelicals on board in 1980. But Francis Schaeffer had been busy expanding concern about abortion through his books and films *How Should We Then Live?* and *Whatever Happened to the Human Race?* Perhaps pressured by Ted Kennedy's primary challenge from the left – Kennedy became the first of many pro-life Democrats to flip to a pro-choice position once they set their eyes on the Oval Office – Carter offered little more than lip service to his conservative Christian critics. Many of the evangelicals who backed Carter in 1976 now wore buttons touting a life amendment and bluntly declaring, "Abort Carter."

Creation Gets Left Behind

During the 1980 presidential election campaign, care for creation was not showing up prominently on most evangelicals' radar, either as an action item or a bogeyman. The National

Association of Evangelicals had called environmental degradation sinful as early as 1970, but there was little mobilization on the issue. While Ron Sider would help launch the Evangelical Environmental Network in the 1990s, the social-justice-focused Chicago Declaration of 1973 that he also coordinated had said nothing about pollution or species extinction, key issues propelling the broader wave of environmentalism.

For its part, the green movement's leadership read Lynn White's famous essay "The Historical Roots of our Ecologic Crisis," which laid the blame for environmental devastation on Christian "dominion" theology. As the Sierra Club's Carl Pope would later lament, "We rejected the churches."

The cannons of the culture war were never meant to obliterate a Christian concern for creation.

Environmentalists also increasingly rejected economic conservatives, and vice versa. Fear of GOP nominee Ronald Reagan, who had aligned himself with the anti-regulatory and pro-development "Sagebrush Rebellion," drove many conservation groups to adopt an "all in with the Dems" strategy. The result was the weakening of bipartisan bridges.

After a convincing win, the new president began what historian Samuel P. Hays somewhat breathlessly called "the Reagan anti-environmental revolution." The solar panels that Carter had installed on the White House roof came down, and a business-backed narrative about the high costs of overregulation increasingly won the day. Although Reagan eventually shifted back toward the center after 1983, the dominos had already been set in motion. Even his undeniably green efforts like spearheading the Montreal Protocol, an international treaty to preserve the ozone layer, would not garner laurels from embittered environmentalists until decades later.

In short, concern about abortion and other moral issues sent evangelicals towards an increasingly welcoming GOP, while a tough-talking Reagan sent environmentalists running the other direction. In 1980, the average Republican House member scored about 40 percent from the League of Conservation Voters; the average Democrat was just a bit better at 50 percent. By the year 2000, Democrats were scoring 80 percent while Republicans had fallen to around 15 percent, and in recent years the split has approached 90 to 10.

Exit polls tell a similar tale on abortion. The average Democratic voter was actually slightly more pro-life than the average Republican in 1980. Soon thereafter, though, a steady divergence set in as pro-lifers moved to the GOP camp. The number of pro-life Democrats in the House has fallen from upwards of one hundred in 1976 to the single digits today.

Currently, those interested in protecting babies in the womb *and* the world into which these babies will be born get pushed into a political no man's land, taking mortar fire from both sides. Ask Al Gore about how he squares his "choose life" language on climate change with his support of *Roe,* and you might find yourself being verbally accosted by his chief of staff. Blog on one conservative site that Gore does raise a valid scientific point or two, and get ready to be labeled the "idiot of the day" on another.

Meanwhile, Christian conservatives just helped to return the Senate to a party led by one happy to identify himself as a "friend of coal," yet campaigning Republicans showed far less enthusiasm towards marriage and unborn life. Is this our reward for thirty-five years of loyalty: mountaintop removal mining and membership

in the "it's a hoax" club? Would anyone have struck this bargain in 1980?

It bears repeating that the current partisan dividing lines were hardly inevitable. In fact, it would seem quite logical for the party of the little guy to champion the littlest guys and gals, or for conservatives to stand up for conservation.

Thanks to Francis, and Francis

The smoke has cleared a bit from the days when climate change was the top media obsession, and the relative calm presents an opportunity for broader reflection on the role of Christians as global and cultural caretakers. It's both timely and heartening, then, that Pope Francis has announced the 2015 release of an environmental encyclical. With this step, he will be continuing the tradition of both family- and earth-friendly exhortations that flowed from his recent predecessors. Consider Pope Benedict XVI's words in *Caritas in Veritate:* "Our duties toward the environment are linked to our duties toward the human person, considered in himself and in relation to others. It would be wrong to uphold one set of duties while trampling on the other." The legacy of Benedict, the very pro-life "Green Pope" who brought solar energy to the Vatican, seems to imply that we should care for the unborn in the womb, the communities they will be born into, and for the world that will be theirs to steward after we are gone. You don't have to believe in papal infallibility to hear that as pretty good advice.

Evangelicals have no popes, but the man whom a 1997 *Christianity Today* cover declared to be "Our Saint Francis" does loom large in recent history. Schaeffer, who died in 1984, helped to load the cannons of the culture war, but they were never meant to obliterate a Christian concern for creation. All along he knew that the church had a bigger role than just being a reliable party precinct. In *Christian Manifesto,* one of his final works, Schaeffer warned, "We should not wrap Christianity in our national flag," and the same could be said of a party label. Christians are called to find our identity first and foremost in Christ and the kingdom of God, regardless of how much that matches or conflicts with a political platform.

The church, as Schaeffer urged in *Pollution and the Death of Man,* should be striving to be a "pilot plant" demonstrating to the world (including its flawed political institutions) the possibility of "substantial healing in every area affected by the Fall." Regarding the breach between humanity and the rest of creation, Schaeffer said believers should "exercise dominion over nature without being destructive," and he wanted to see the situation he experienced at the ravine reversed: Christians should outshine the pagans in the care of the earth. Schaeffer feared that "unless something like this happens, I do not believe the world will listen to what we have to say."

A Way Forward

Echoing Schaeffer, how should we then live? Upstream from politics, the first step may well be to get our own houses in order. Personal, family, and community life matters. The decisions we make about how we feed our families, fuel our locomotion, and fashion our sense of the good life may seem inconsequential in the face of worldwide environmental problems. Yet by embracing local particulars we begin to free ourselves from the despair of global abstraction.

One place to start is at the table. To some it may seem surprising that Joel Salatin, the hero of Michael Pollan's bestseller *The Omnivore's Dilemma* and films such as the Oscar-nominated *Food, Inc.,* is a man of deep Christian faith whose politics hardly match those of the left. The slow foodies' favorite farmer does his work rooted in a love of his family, of the land and animals entrusted to him, and ultimately of the Creator of it all.

Edmund Burke, the eighteenth-century father of conservatism, spoke of loving "the little platoon we belong to in society" as "the first principle (the germ as it were) of public affections." A very Burkean Roger Scruton describes this as *oikophilia,* or the love of home, and he sees it as a necessary motivation above and beyond the libertarian focus on rational self-interest. Admirers of the American farmer-philosopher-poet Wendell Berry will no doubt be familiar with such thinking as well. Upon receiving one of our nation's highest honors in the humanities, Berry entitled his Jefferson Lecture "It All Turns on Affection."

The gospel is good news for all of the world that God so loved.

Our churches can play a role, too, both in word and deed. The gospel is good news for all of the world that God so loved, but the Christ who reconciles "all things" is too often reduced to a Star Trek–style savior who will teleport us away to a wispy heaven. N.T. Wright, the New Testament scholar, writes of Romans 8 that "when humans are put right, creation will be put right." We need a cosmic vision of salvation, one that does not jettison personal redemption but expands it. Better proclamation is key, to be sure, but there is also a very material aspect to becoming the "pilot plant" that Schaeffer urged as essential. The intentional cultivation of beauty plays an important role, as was seen in Schaeffer's ravine story. So do things that are less obvious, like insulation and LED lighting.

Kingdom and Democracy

Can we then just ignore politics if we hike the Appalachian Trail, switch to pastured eggs and grass-fed beef, wrap our water heater, and put solar panels on the roof? Not quite. Even if too much emphasis has been put on politics during recent decades, in a democratic republic Christians do not have the option of simply washing their hands of public affairs.

Of course, the relationship of Christians to politics has often been a point of friction between Anabaptists and the more politically engaged wings of Christianity. Some would argue that we serve Christ better by being "the quiet in the land" rather than by putting signs in our hands. Perhaps the tension is overstated, though. Ron Sider, for example, has spent decades as an Anabaptist activist, and has done so without contorting his beliefs to toe a party line. Operating primarily in political circles on the left, the founder of Evangelicals for Social Action has nevertheless continued to affirm the importance of things such as evangelism, unborn life, and traditional marriage. Though one may disagree with some of Sider's political priorities and policy suggestions, his witness bespeaks a man striving first for fidelity to the kingdom, not a party.

Sider told *Christianity Today* in 1992 of a trip to Switzerland he initiated after being criticized by the post-Schaeffer leadership at L'Abri. Unable to crack their perception that he was a dangerous man, an exasperated Sider later lamented, "Francis Schaeffer – I'm so *close* to him!" At least on the protection of unborn children and the care of creation, the views of the godfather of the evangelical left and the godfather of the religious right were indeed rather close. It is time for their political progeny to get close again. Instead of arm-wrestling with itself, the body of Christ should be extending both hands to a broken culture and a broken creation.

Letter from Charleston

PETE MEIER

Where Rivers Meet the Sea

The Fragile Beauty of Marine Estuaries

Photograph by Sandy L. Kirkner / Getty Images

It's a gray January day, the warmth of the summer sun now a distant memory. As I throttle up the engine and push the *R/V Chamberlain* out of the boat slip, we are met by a brisk northeast wind and whitecaps breaking over the windshield. We are out collecting oyster samples to bring back to the lab for analysis – a wet and muddy chore, but a worthwhile one. A sentinel species, these lowly creatures are a valuable indicator of the health of a marine ecosystem. As filter-feeding organisms, they help control pollution; a single oyster can filter around fifty gallons of water in a day, improving water quality for other species.

As we leave the harbor and nudge up a tidal creek to our first collection site, the smell of the marsh greets us – that glorious low-tide smell, a blend of seaweed, salt, and mud that few but a marine scientist can truly love. The smell of life.

Estuaries – where a long arm of the sea reaches inland to meet the mouth of a river – are among the most ecologically rich places on earth. Since they offer both abundant food and protection from the harshness of the open

Photograph courtesy of Pete Meier

ocean, they provide a habitat for a vast variety of marine animals. As "nurseries of the sea," they are a haven where many species of fish and marine invertebrates produce their offspring; here the young can mature in relative safety before returning to the deep water. Meanwhile the salt marshes and oyster beds that fringe the estuaries act as giant filtration systems, sequestering nutrients and degrading pollutants. They also protect shorelines from erosion by wind and waves.

Human civilization was born on estuaries for similar reasons: safe harbors for boats and bounteous water and food. The earliest known urban development began around the Euphrates River estuary in the city of Ur, in what is now Iraq. Similarly, early Egyptians depended on the Nile River estuary for trade, agriculture, and fish.

Modernity has rewarded the openhandedness of estuary ecosystems with destruction. Expanding cities are driving land reclamation projects around the globe, dredging and depositing sand and silt and obliterating salt marshes. This upsets the fragile ecological balance, decimating fish populations and destabilizing the land-sea interface, as dramatically illustrated by Hurricane Katrina in the Mississippi Delta and Hurricane Sandy in the Northeast. In addition, ships routinely spill sewage, ballast water, and fuel into estuary ports; propeller wash and port dredging devastate habitats on the estuary floor and re-suspend deposited toxins.

How can this unique natural world get better treatment from humans? Education is a vital first step. I count myself fortunate to be able to share my passion for marine science with local schools here in Charleston, South Carolina. The marine-biology students I work with trace their love of the ocean back to childhood trips to the beach or to boating and fishing in local estuaries. As more people discover the joys of kayaking, fishing, or bird watching, public awareness is growing that as stewards of this blue planet, we must protect these environments for future generations.

As I end this day in my office, wrapping up some paperwork, my mind turns to the coming summer, when I can slip out at dusk in my kayak, fishing rod in hand, with only a thin layer of fiberglass separating me from the water and all that lives beneath, to explore the miles of tidal creeks and salt marshes that I love. An egret fishing for dinner, the click and clack of armies of fiddler crabs scurrying through the marsh grass, a school of silvery mullet breaking through the glassy surface, chased by an unseen predator – all these, and that intoxicating low-tide smell.

Pete Meier is marine operations manager for the College of Charleston's Grice Marine Laboratory in Charleston, South Carolina.

GET INVOLVED:

There are encouraging signs of recovery and progress in the restoration of some estuary ecosystems. Community-based groups up and down the eastern seaboard of the United States are working to clean up wetlands, restore historic oyster beds, and replant *Spartina,* the primary grass that naturally inhabits salt marshes. To help with reclamation efforts, contact your state's natural resources agency. If you live in South Carolina, I would be happy to arrange for groups to join us in our oyster reef restoration project. *www.gricemarinelab.cofc.edu*

CALVIN B. DEWITT

The Psalmic Soundtrack

Singing from Two Books

Above, Dunbar Castle, whose walls the young Muir scaled in his introduction to mountaineering.

Would I ever read it? Another volume from a natural history book club had arrived in the mail. Month after month they came, but I was so engaged in doing natural history that I read none of them. A few decades later, with more time to spare in my Wisconsin home on peaceful Waubesa Wetlands, I finally picked the volume off the shelf and began to read John Muir. As I turned the pages, I soon found myself caught up in a psalmic crescendo. It was not only Muir's lyrical writing but also the familiar soundtrack playing in the background. Ever present, it occasionally surfaced in visible text but more often rung in resonating allusions – ever present, always playing. This soundtrack, I was to discover, was one by which he lived, moved, and had his being.

Since then I have enjoyed other Muir books, along with his extensive personal correspondence, available at the Wisconsin Historical Society. In fact, my enthusiasm led me to visit his boyhood home at the edge of the wild North Sea on the southeast coast of Scotland. He was

Calvin B. DeWitt is a professor of environmental studies at the University of Wisconsin–Madison and co-founder of the Evangelical Environmental Network. This essay was adapted by him from his book Song of a Scientist: The Harmony of a God-Soaked Creation *(Square Inch Books, 2012).*

Photograph by Richard Paxman

# of John Muir

born here on April 21, 1838. Sixteen days later, he was baptized in Dunbar's Ebenezer Erskine Memorial Church, a secessionist congregation that had broken from the state-controlled church. In his earliest years grandfather David Gilrye taught him to read the letters on signs across the street, and at age three Johnnie was enrolled in school. He soon found that he "was fond of everything that was wild."

"Fortunately around my native town of Dunbar, by the stormy North Sea, there was no lack of wildness," he would write later. "I loved to wander in the fields to hear the birds sing, and along the seashore to gaze and wonder at the shells and seaweeds, eels and crabs in the pools among the rocks when the tide was low; and best of all to watch the waves in awful storms thundering on the black headlands and craggy ruins of the old Dunbar Castle when the sea and the sky, the waves and the clouds, were mingled together as one." His introduction to mountaineering came from scaling this castle's crumbling red bricks with his chums.

Here also Muir's soundtrack was instilled in him from early childhood: that of the Psalms, whose earliest strains had emerged more than three thousand years before. In Dunbar, the young Muir grew up within a rich Scottish milieu of devout psalm-singing. This practice stemmed from re-introduction of congregational singing in the mid-1500s in the city-state of Geneva, where texts were put into rhymed verse and fitted with syllabic homophony, making them singable and hummable by anyone who could carry a tune. From Geneva, the psalter entered Muir's native Scotland. Meanwhile, psalm singing in the Low Countries was advanced by the *Dutch Psalter,* a songbook that later inspired the *Psalter Hymnal* in America.

The Scottish psalter's full title was *The Psalms of David in Metre with Notes by John Brown of Haddington.* Reverend Brown's prefatory note to each psalm links it with its New Testament fulfillment in Christ, gifting its singers with a wide embrace of the scriptures. For example, the versification of Psalm 19, "The heav'ns God's glory do declare, the skies his hand-works preach . . . ," is prefaced by this note:

> Now the books of God are opened, not for my trial and condemnation in the last judgment, but for my instruction. Let my soul look and read therein –
>
> 1. The book of creation and providence, in which all the works of God instruct mankind in general, concerning the eternal wisdom, power, and goodness of their Maker, verses 1–6.

2. The book of inspiration; the sure, the right, the pure, the true, the perfect and powerful oracles of which instruct, convert, comfort, and warm the members of the church; and in keeping of which there is an exceeding great and everlasting reward of glory obtained, verses 7–11.
3. What conviction of sin! What supplication for pardon of it, and preservation from it, and for the acceptance of our duties through Jesus' blood, doth or ought to ensue upon a proper perusal of these volumes of heaven, verses 12–14. . . .

These two books – the book of nature, and the Bible – are mentioned as well in the catechism of the Scottish churches – the Westminster Shorter Catechism – no doubt memorized by young Johnnie. The catechism's third question: "In what volumes has God discovered the knowledge of himself to all mankind?" The answer: "In the great volumes of creation and providence; which he opens to all the world." And Question 7: "Though the works of creation and providence declare that God is, can they also tell us what God is?" The catechism answers: "They afford us some dark glimpses of his eternal power, wisdom, greatness, and goodness, but it is only by and through the scriptures of truth, set home on the soul by his Spirit, that we can attain the saving knowledge of God, and of his perfections."

Can ye see unmoved the glory of the Almighty?

That Glorious Wilderness

In Dunbar scripture was embedded in young minds very early, so that by the time Muir left Scotland for Wisconsin at age eleven he had memorized the whole New Testament and two-thirds of the Old Testament. The journey to North America came when his father, Daniel, a prosperous Dunbar merchant, sold his house and fine garden in 1849 to seek a place where he could hold strongly to Scottish traditions, stay true to the church universal, and pursue the "Scottish ambition" that fueled a centuries-long "Scottish diaspora." Intending to sail to Canada, he was diverted by fellow Scots who described Wisconsin and Michigan land as good and more easily cultivated. Sailing up the St. Lawrence River, he met a Buffalo grain dealer who got most of his wheat from Wisconsin. So Daniel sailed across the Great Lakes to Milwaukee. Upon arrival he left the children in Kingston (other family members were still in Scotland), scouted the land, and found a place where he built a little shanty with "rough bur-oak logs for the walls and white-oak boards for the floor and roof." Next, he picked up the children and went by "ox-team across trackless carex swamps and low rolling hills sparely dotted with round-headed oaks." Later John would write, "Here without knowing it we were still at school; every wild lesson a love lesson, not whipped but charmed into us. Oh, that glorious Wisconsin wilderness!"

From his youth John believed that both books should be seriously read. Taking to heart Matthew 6:26, he told of Sundays at his Wisconsin home:

> After or before chores and sermons and Bible lessons, we drifted about on the lake for hours, especially in lily time, getting finest lessons and sermons from the water and flowers, ducks, fishes, and muskrats. In particular we took Christ's advice and devoutly "considered the lilies" – how they grow up in beauty out of gray lime mud, and ride gloriously among the breezy sun-spangles. On our way home we gathered grand bouquets of them to be

> kept fresh all the week. No flower was hailed with greater wonder and admiration by the European settlers . . . than this white water lily (*Nymphaea odorata*). It is a magnificent plant, queen of the inland waters, pure white, three or four inches in diameter, the most beautiful, sumptuous, and deliciously fragrant of all our Wisconsin flowers.

Leaving home, Muir spent two and a half years as a student at the University of Wisconsin, then worked briefly in an Indiana machine shop as an inventor until a serious accident temporarily blinded him. Deeply thankful to recover his eyesight, he decided to behold "the inventions of God," inaugurating what would become a lifelong journey with a thousand-mile walk to the Gulf of Mexico. In his backpack he carried a copy of the New Testament – even though he had committed it to heart – alongside Milton's *Paradise Lost* and a book of Robert Burns' poetry. Coming to where "the view extends from the Cumberland Mountains on the north far into Georgia and North Carolina to the south," he beheld "countless forest-clad hills, side by side in rows and groups" that seemed "to be enjoying the rich sunshine and remaining motionless only because they were so eagerly absorbing it. All were united by curves and slopes of inimitable softness and beauty. What perfection, what divinity, in their architecture! What simplicity and mysterious complexity of detail!" Ever holding in his heart the metaphor of nature as a book, he continues, "Who shall read the teaching of these sylvan pages, the glad brotherhood of rills that sing in the valleys, and all the happy creatures that dwell in them under the tender keeping of a Father's care?"

John Muir, 1907

Photograph by Francis M. Fritz. Courtesy of UC Berkeley, Bancroft Library.

John Muir's coherent reading of the pages of nature and scripture – within each and between – is richly present in a letter written from Yosemite in 1870, at age 32, to his brother David Gilrye Muir, in which he exalts, "This glorious valley might well be called a church, for every lover of the great Creator who comes within the broad overwhelming influences of the place fails not to worship as he never did before." Alluding to Isaiah 6:3, he exclaims, "The glory of the Lord is upon all his works; it is written plainly upon all the fields of every clime, and upon every sky, but here in this place of surpassing glory the Lord has written in capitals." And he hopes for David ". . . that one day you will see and read with your own eyes."

Reflecting on California's Mono Lake – a place "generally described as a dreary forbidding waste" – Muir wrote in a letter to Emily O. Pelton, also in 1870: "I never beheld a place where beauty was written in plainer characters or where the tender fostering hand of the Great Gardener was more directly visible."

But the book of creation and providence is not only a book for reading or beholding. It also is a book for *listening*, for it is speaking, even *proclaiming*, Muir insists. "We seem to imagine that since Herod beheaded John the Baptist, there is no longer any voice crying in

Gloria in excelsis

JOHN MUIR

Photograph by Russell Sipe

The East Side of the Fairweather Mountains

After we had seen the unveiling of the majestic peaks and glaciers that evening, and their baptism in the down-pouring sunbeams, it was inconceivable that nature could have anything finer to show us. Nevertheless, compared with what was coming the next morning, all that was as nothing. As far as we could see, the lovely dawn gave no promise of anything uncommon. Its most impressive features were the frosty clearness of the sky, and a deep, brooding calm, made all the more striking by the intermittent thunder of the bergs. The sunrise we did not see at all, for we were beneath the shadows of the fiord cliffs; but in the midst of our studies we were startled by the sudden appearance of a red light burning with a strange, unearthly splendor on the topmost peak of the Fairweather Mountains. Instead of vanishing as suddenly as it had appeared, it spread and spread until the whole range down to the level of the glaciers was filled with the celestial fire. In color it was at first a vivid crimson, with a thick, furred appearance, as fine as the alpenglow, yet indescribably rich and deep – not in the least like a garment or mere external flush or bloom through which one might expect to see the rocks or snow, but every mountain apparently glowing from the heart like molten metal fresh from a furnace. Beneath the frosty shadows of the fiord we stood hushed and awe-stricken, gazing at the holy vision; and had we seen the heavens open and God made manifest, our attention could not have been more tremendously strained. When the highest peak began to burn, it did not seem to be steeped in sunshine, however glorious, but rather as if it had been thrust into the body of the sun itself. Then the supernal fire slowly descending, with a sharp line of demarcation separating it from the cold, shaded region beneath, peak after peak, with their spires and ridges and cascading glaciers, caught the heavenly glow, until all the mighty host stood transfigured, hushed, and thoughtful, as if awaiting the coming of the Lord. The white, rayless light of the morning, seen when I was alone amid the silent peaks of the Sierra, had always seemed to me the most telling of the terrestrial manifestations of God. But here the mountains themselves were made divine, and declared his glory in terms still more impressive. How long we gazed I never knew.

The mountains themselves declared God's glory.

Taken from John Muir, "The Discovery of Glacier Bay," in The Century *50(2):239.*

the wilderness," he writes. "But no one in the wilderness can possibly make such a mistake, for every one of these flowers is such a voice. No wilderness in the world is so desolate as to be without divine ministers. God's love covers all the earth as the sky covers it, and also fills it in every pore. And this love has voices heard by all who have ears to hear." Like John the Baptist announcing the coming of the Lord, the mountains echo angelic strains in joyful praise: *Gloria in excelsis Deo!* So also does John Muir of the mountains hear heaven and nature sing – above, around, and o'er the plains – and he exuberantly echoes its sounding joy.

So who do people say Muir is? "Was he a transcendentalist, a pantheist, a deist, a theist?" asks biologist Raymond Barnett. In the journal *Religions* he writes, "Most of those attempting to categorize Muir have been scholars of history, literature, or religious studies. As a scientist and modest mountaineer, it strikes me that the Muir biographies by Wolfe, Wilkins, Worster, Cohen, and Turner somehow do not sufficiently credit Muir as the accomplished scientist that he was, nor how incredible his mountaineering feats were, in his time or ours." More importantly, Barnett also says that "a simple reading of his writings convinces me that in fact Muir must be recognized as the Christian that he was. His writings are full of references to God and quotations from both the Old and the New Testaments . . . and Muir finds this Christian framework adequate to express his convictions."

Seeing God's Smile

The year 2014 marked the hundredth anniversary of John Muir's passing. The distance between his time and ours raises questions in some minds about his relevance to the world as we know it. In answer to such questions we may well ask whether it remains worthwhile to read and listen to the book of nature. Is it worth our time and attention – as it was for John Muir one hundred years ago and King David three thousand years ago – to engage in looking, beholding, and listening, with eyes and heart? We would also do well to consider everything we have placed in the way to block out nature's psalmic testimony.

In a letter to Mr. and Mrs. David M. Galloway in 1863, Muir describes beholding the Wisconsin Dells – a stretch of narrows on the Wisconsin River some twenty miles west of his boyhood home:

> The banks are rocky and romantic for many miles both above and below the Dells. On going up the river we were delightfully opposed and threatened by a great many semi-gorge ravines running at right angles to the river. . . . Those ravines are the most perfect, the most heavenly plant conservatories I ever saw. . . . The last ravine we encountered was the most beautiful and deepest and longest and narrowest. The rocks overhang and bear a perfect selection of trees which hold themselves towards one another from side to side with inimitable grace, forming a flower-veil of indescribable beauty. The light is measured and mellowed. For every flower springs, too, and pools, are there in their places to moisten them. The walls are fringed and painted most divinely with the bright green polypodium and asplenium and mosses and liverworts with gray lichens, and here and there a clump of flowers and little bushes. The floor was barred and banded and sheltered by bossy, shining, moss-clad logs cast in as needed from above. Over all and above all and in all the glorious ferns, tall, perfect, godlike, and here and there amid their fronds a long cylindrical spike of the grand fringed purple orchis.

Today, we can access *wisdells.com* to find the Wisconsin Dells billed as "The Waterpark Capital of the World!®" and that "our world-famous indoor waterparks aren't the only reason to visit. As one of the most popular Wisconsin vacation spots, there are many other reasons to love the Dells this time of year [winter]. Like live entertainment, thrilling attractions, lux to cozy accommodations, and dining options to please any palate." The Dells area is now advertised as a major amusement park, and it lives up to the following definitions of "amuse" given by the Oxford English Dictionary: "To divert the attention of any one from the facts at issue; to beguile, delude, cheat, deceive. . . . To divert the attention of (one) from serious business by anything trifling, ludicrous, or entertaining."

Yosemite National Park, California

Wrapping up either of the two books in the glitter of "amusements" intercepts and mutes the testimony and redeeming message of both. And so too the testimony and redeeming message of John Muir – and other serious readers of both books – can be intercepted and muted in ways that prevent others from seeing through to his heart. It is as John Muir's close friend and publisher, Robert Underwood Johnson, wrote in a remembrance in the *Sierra Club Bulletin* of 1916: "To some, beauty seems but an accident of creation: to Muir it was the very smile of God. He sung the glory of nature like another Psalmist, and, as a true artist, was unashamed of his emotions. An instance of this is told of him as he stood with an acquaintance at one of the great view-points of the Yosemite Valley and, filled with wonder and devotion, wept. His companion, more stolid than most,

Photograph by Darvin Atkeson, *YosemiteLandscapes.com*

could not understand his feeling, and was so thoughtless as to say so. 'Mon,' said Muir, with the Scotch dialect into which he often lapsed, 'Can ye see unmoved the glory of the Almighty?'

"'Oh, it's very fine,' was the reply, 'but I do not wear my heart upon my sleeve.'

"'Ah, my dear mon,' said Muir, 'In the face of such a scene as this, it's no time to be thinkin' o' where to wear your heart.'"

Nature and Revelation

Caspar David Friedrich's *Cross in the Mountains*

ELIZABETH LEV

"The God who made the world and everything in it, he who is Lord of heaven and earth, does not live in shrines made by hands" (Acts 17:24).

In the history of art, creating a locus for the Lord has remained a ceaseless challenge. Byzantine mosaicists placed him against a golden background outside of space and time; Renaissance painters contained him in perfect perspectival order. In Caspar David Friedrich's 1807 altarpiece, *Cross in the Mountains,* for the first time God was revealed in untamed landscape.

Landscape paintings were well known and avidly collected by the nineteenth century, but considered a lesser art form, without the prestige of paintings of historical subjects. The European artistic tradition dictated that any kind of natural setting for the sacred must be clearly dominated by man – hence the dense swards of Leonardo da Vinci and the idealized vistas of Claude Lorrain. Friedrich, unveiling this work in his Dresden studio, sparked a controversy that would force contemporaries to rethink not only art criticism, but also the evocation of the divine.

Friedrich intended *Cross in the Mountains* as a gift to Gustav IV Adolf, king of Sweden, an erratic but devout monarch. With the king, the artist shared an affinity for the Moravian Brethren, for whom faith was, as their founder Count Zinzendorf wrote, "not in thoughts nor in the head, but . . . a light illuminated in the heart."* The painting reflects both love of a rugged homeland and a deeply personal faith.

* Joseph Leo Koerner, *Caspar David Friedrich and the Subject of Landscape* (Reaktion Books, 2009), 60.

Cross in the Mountains depicts a Gipfelkreuz, one of the "summit crosses" that have been erected on mountain peaks in the Alps since the thirteenth century, especially in Catholic regions. The cross is placed off-center, a slender naked reed among the densely clad fir trees that flank the mountaintop. The body on the cross turns away from the viewer – something impossible in medieval art and rare in Renaissance works, but not an unknown convention during the Baroque era. The viewer gazes from behind and slightly to the right, as if standing by the lone tree low on the rocky slope.

From the shadows, the viewer lifts his eyes to Christ who reflects light with a polished gleam. The image not only draws one to the light of Christ, but instills a longing to be in the line of his gaze and within the sweep of his outstretched arms.

What lies on the other side of the slope, one wonders? Friedrich has left but a few clues. The trees seem more than just a random scattering; with their tall erect trunks they appear to climb towards the cross with their upturned branches lifted in praise. It is as if the forest itself recognizes in the spent body on the cross's denuded wood the Master of heaven and earth. The delicate tendril of evergreen ivy climbing up the foot of the cross recalls that human frailty was conquered by Christ, who defeated death itself.

The viewer knows that below the harsh and rocky mountaintop come pastures and villages, and further down, cities which group into nations. When Friedrich painted this work in 1807, war was raging throughout Europe. The Enlightenment, which had promised rationality

© Staatliche Kunstsammlungen Dresden / Bridgeman Images

Caspar David Friedrich, *Cross in the Mountains,* oil on canvas, Galerie Neue Meister, Dresden, Germany

Caspar David Friedrich on his painting:
"Jesus Christ, nailed to the tree, is turned here towards the setting sun, the image of the eternal life-giving father. With Jesus' teaching, an old world dies – that time when God and Father moved directly on earth. This sun sank and the earth was not able to grasp the departing light any longer. There shines forth in the gold of the evening light the purest, noblest metal of the Savior's figure on the cross, which thus reflects on earth in a softened glow. The cross stands erected on a rock, unshakably firm like our faith in Jesus Christ. The firs stand around the cross, evergreen enduring through all ages, like the hopes of man in Him, the crucified."

A Social History of Modern Art, 2 (University of Chicago Press, 1991)

From WikiArt (public domain)

Caspar David Friedrich, *Hill and Ploughed Field near Dresden*

and liberty for humankind, had dissolved into conflict. Friedrich sought refuge from the violence of his age not in painting the exploits of great men, but in the quiet of nature – terrible and awesome, but without malice.

The one element of artifice in this work is the play of light. The bright wings of the scene gather into thick tumultuous clouds that range from grey-violet to startling pink, stretching from the viewer's space to the other side of the slopes. Three shafts of light launch into the clouds, but cannot penetrate the dense cumulus. Friedrich described them as the setting sun, perhaps symbolizing the loss of the time when God walked among human beings, or perhaps the dimming of the Enlightenment or even the end of a pagan past.

One ray, however, strikes the body of Christ. Jesus mediates between this dark and light, a meeting between our search for clarity and the mystery of our final destiny. He is the invisible made visible. Serene skies hint at a hope for peace, while the mountain, which at first appears as an obstacle, slowly becomes the anchor of the work, the embodiment of steadfast faith.

The frame, designed by Friedrich himself, gives a more formal setting to the rugged scene. The classical arch crowning Christ is formed by palm fronds, age-old symbols of victory, while the heads of cherubim and seraphim look down at the scene. The predella is designed with a sheaf of wheat and a vine encircling the all-seeing eye of God. Jesus on the cross gazes away from us, but the eye of God, framed by symbols of the Eucharist, stares directly at the viewer.

Confined in its heavily symbolic cornice, the painting takes on a more recognizable religious meaning fitting for a sacred space. But viewed alone, the works offers an iconography that can speak to all Christians: shadow becomes light, and nature both hinders and guides us with its grandeur. In this way, Friedrich's work recalls the poetry of Saint Francis, whose "Canticle of the Creatures" praises God as he is reflected in his creation:

> Praised be you, my Lord,
> with all your creatures,
> especially Sir Brother Sun. . . .
> He bears a likeness of You, Most High One.

Elizabeth Lev teaches Christian art and architecture at Duquesne University's Rome campus.

Digging Deeper

A Reading List on Earth and the Environment

Must-Reads: Wendell Berry's *The Art of the Common Place* exhorts readers to return to the land in order to become "at home" in the world and find wisdom, peace, and well-being. "Agrarianism . . . promises a path toward wholeness with the earth, with each other, and with God, a path founded upon an insight into our proper place within the wider universe." The needs of the natural and human communities that sustain us must take precedence over our selfish desires, transforming us from exploiters into nurturers.

Travelling through Italy, Egypt, and the Holy Land in the footsteps of Saint Francis, Ernest Raymond captures the beautiful and intimate connection Francis had with the world surrounding him. *In the Steps of St. Francis* includes Francis' "Sermon to the Birds" and "Canticle of the Sun," which express the love he had for the Creator and his creation. As Raymond writes, "Here, among the thistles and the stones, were moments of communion, illumination, and knowledge that are of greater importance to our race than the most heralded discoveries of science." Francis' impact on science, art, literature, and religion have established him as patron saint of the environment.

American Earth is an anthology of the environmental writings of authors ranging from Henry David Thoreau to Rebecca Solnit. Included in this volume are prominent authors and activists from the 1800s to the present. The writings of historical giants such as John Muir and Rachel Carson share space with more contemporary voices such as Wendell Berry and Paul Hawken, compiled by Bill McKibben into what is possibly the most comprehensive synthesis of environmental literature of the century.

Recommended: In his heartwarming and heartbreaking collection, *Arctic Voices,* Subhankar Banerjee compiles thirty-nine descriptive essays and accounts by environmental activists. This collection deliberates the Arctic's natural diversity and beauty, and how it has been exploited and poisoned for decades, endangering the people, plants, and animals that live there. Banerjee shows how climate change in the Far North is interconnected with the places where the rest of us live. These essays demand that we reconsider the environmental war we are waging on our only home.

In the twenty essays of his book, *The Soul of the Night,* Chet Raymo blends cosmology, astronomy, literature, physics, anthropology, history, mythology, carbon atoms, mourning cloaks, and quasars in his search for knowledge of, and faith in, the invisible Creator. "The pilgrimage is one that each of us must take alone, into the realm of the stars and galaxies, to the limits of the universe, to that boundary of space and time where the mind and heart encounter the ultimate mystery, the known unknowable." For those seeking to gain a deeper understanding of the interconnectivity of science and spirit, this book is a must.

Elizabeth Kolbert's reporting about ecosystems and species presents a challenging view of the sixth major extinction happening before our eyes. Her book, *The Sixth Extinction,* describes the details of this approaching apocalypse and paints a vivid global picture of the end of an epoch. Ours. "I try to convey both sides: the excitement of what's being learned as well as the horror of it," writes Kolbert. "My hope is that readers of this book will come away with an appreciation of the truly extraordinary moment in which we live."

Must-Reads

The Art of the Commonplace
The Agrarian Essays of Wendell Berry
Ed. Norman Wirza
(Counterpoint)

In the Steps of St. Francis
Ernest Raymond
(Franciscan Herald Press)

American Earth
Environmental Writing Since Thoreau
Ed. Bill McKibben
(Library of America)

Recommended

Arctic Voices
Resistance at the Tipping Point
Ed. Subhankar Banerjee
(Seven Stories Press)

The Soul of the Night
An Astronomical Pilgrimage
Chet Raymo
(Hungry Mind Press)

The Sixth Extinction
An Unnatural History
Elizabeth Kolbert
(Henry Holt & Company)

The White Lily

Jane Tyson Clement

Adapted from Frances Jenkins Olcott
Illustrated by Hannah Marsden

NCE LONG AGO, near a village far away, there lived an old peasant known as Ivan. He had a little hut, a small garden, a dog named Rubles, and a six-year-old nephew, Peter, who was an orphan. Ivan was not a bad man, as he did not murder, did not steal, told no lies, and did not meddle in other people's business. But on the other hand he couldn't be called a good man either. He was cross and dirty. He seldom spoke, and then only grudgingly and unpleasantly. He paid no attention to his neighbors, never showed them kindness, and refused any small courtesy or friendliness they offered him. Eventually they paid no attention to him either and let him go his own way. As for Rubles the dog, he was afraid of his master and never went near him. He would follow him at a distance to the village and back, would bark at all strangers as watch-dogs should do, and he would drive off the foxes that tried to molest the hens. So Ivan kept the dog and left scraps for him, but never stroked or praised him.

Peter was a silent little boy, since he was never spoken to except in anger. He had no friends, for the village children feared his uncle too much to come near him, and Peter was too shy to speak to anyone. So he ran wild in the woods and made up his own lonely games. He feared his uncle Ivan, who had never beaten him hard but had laid a stick to him now and then, and who spoke to him so fiercely that Peter was quite cowed and frightened.

All this was bad enough, but added to it was filth and ugliness. The little cottage was brown and bleak, the windows (there were two quite nice ones) grimy and stained, the wooden rafters sooty, and all the walls and corners full of cobwebs. On the floor were the scraps and leavings of many meals, and the mud dragged in from many rainy months. The hearth was black, the pots and kettles dingy, the big bed for Ivan and the trundle bed for Peter tumbled and unmade, the table littered and smeared, and the chairs half-broken. It was all a sorry sight, and no better outdoors, for the doorsill was tumbledown, weeds grew everywhere, the vegetables came up as best they might, and not a flower was to be seen.

The living things themselves were even worse. Rubles was thin and dirty and full of burrs. Poor Peter wore rags, his hair grew long and was tangled with straw from his bed, and he was so filthy one could scarcely see the boy beneath. As for Ivan, he was huge. His black hair and beard were unkempt, and he looked quite terrifying. His clothes were as black with age and no washings as his hair. He was so unpleasant to look at that all he met turned their heads away, wrinkled their noses, and passed him as quickly as possible.

One bleak March day, when it seemed as if all had been waiting for spring for many weeks, Ivan had to go to the village to fetch some beans. As he trudged along the road, homeward bound again, in the distance he saw a man coming toward him. Ivan was ready as usual to pass him by without a glance, but when he drew nearer, out of the tail of his eye Ivan noticed he was a stranger, and in spite of himself Ivan looked full at him. Then he could not look away. The stranger was young, tall and spare, in rough peasant dress, with a shepherd's staff. On one arm he carried a sheaf of white lilies, like the day lilies that grew wild in the fields, only so fair and glowing that they dazzled the eye. Ivan stopped in his tracks, and with a smile the stranger stopped also. While Ivan stared, the stranger looked him over slowly, from his broken boots to his lined and dirty face. Then he spoke:

"Good day, friend."

When there was only silence, with Ivan staring, the stranger spoke again.

"What is it you see?"

Ivan lifted his eyes then to the man's face. The light there was like the lilies, and he looked at them again.

"Those flowers . . . I never saw any so fair."

"One of them is yours," said the stranger.

"Mine?" said Ivan.

The stranger took one of them and offered it to Ivan, who with astonishment and unbelief exclaimed, "What do you want for it? I am a poor man."

"I want nothing in return, only that you should keep the flower clean and pure."

Ivan wiped his dirty hands on his coat and reached for the lily. His fingers closed around the stem, and he stood in the road staring at it for a long while, not knowing what to do with the precious thing now that he had it. When he looked up at last, the stranger had passed into the distance again. Carefully Ivan carried the lily home.

Once inside the door he stood doubtfully in the middle of the floor, looking all around at the filth and disorder and not knowing where to put the white shining lily. Peter had been sitting dejectedly by the dead fire, but now he stood up slowly, gazing at his uncle in amazement. At last he found his voice and said to him, "Where did you find it?"

And in a hushed tone Ivan answered, "A stranger gave it to me, for nothing, and told me only to keep it clean and pure. . . . What am I to do with it?"

In an eager voice Peter answered, "We must find something to hold it! On that high shelf you put an empty wine bottle last Easter. That would do."

"Then you must hold it while I fetch the bottle down. But your hands are too dirty! Draw water from the well and wash first!"

This Peter rushed to do, coming back at last with clean hands. Ivan carefully gave him the flower, but cried out when Peter put it to his face to smell it. "Wait! Your face is too dirty!" Ivan seized a rag and rushed outside to the well, where he drew a bucket of water and washed the rag first, and then came in and awkwardly scrubbed Peter's face. When he was through he stepped back, unbelieving, as the boy with care smelled the white flower. He thought he had never seen that boy before. Then he remembered the bottle and clambered up to get it. But it was dirty, too, and clogged with cobwebs. So out to the well it went, and came in clean and shining, filled with clear water. He set the lily in it and placed it on the windowsill. Then they both looked at it. Its glow lit the dim and dingy room, and as they looked at it a wonder rose in Ivan at all the filth around him. "This fair lily cannot live in such a place!" he said aloud. "I must clean it."

"Can I help?" asked Peter.

It was a hard task and took more than one day. Windows were washed, walls and floors swept and scrubbed, pots and kettles scoured, and chairs mended. The table was washed, the beds aired and beaten and put in order, and the hearth polished till the long-neglected tiles gleamed in the firelight and the pots and kettles winked back. The unaccustomed daylight flooded in the windows and the dark rafters shone in the shadows. All the while the lily glowed on the windowsill. When they were done, they looked about them in wonder and pleasure that the little house could be so fair. And then they saw each other.

"We don't belong in a house like this!" said Ivan. "Next we scrub ourselves."

By now he and the boy were friends, having worked so well together. So they scrubbed themselves, and Ivan went to the village to buy decent clothes for them both. He noticed Rubles following him at a distance. When he came home he thought to himself, "That dog is a sight, dirty and full of burrs. He doesn't belong to this house. He must be cleaned." But when he went to get him, the dog slunk away out of reach and feared to come to him. Ivan

put gentleness into his tone, but it took nearly a day to win the dog, until with Peter's help he could brush him and wash him. After soft words and a good supper, Rubles no longer cowered and whined, but gazed at Ivan with a wondering love in his eyes, and beat his tail on the floor, and licked Ivan's hand. And Ivan felt a strange glow in his heart.

So all was well within. But without? What of the broken sill and the brown tumbled garden thick with last year's weeds? "A house like this cannot live in a garden like that," said Ivan in a cheerful voice. "We must clean it up." So they went to work, while Rubles sat on his haunches to look at them. And a neighbor passing by stopped to watch, perplexed and astounded and scarcely recognizing the two who worked.

"What are you staring at, neighbor?" called Ivan. "Come in to see our lily. But first go fetch your good wife."

And this the neighbor did, in haste and astonishment, eager to be friendly at last to the old man and his little boy.

For seven days the lily glowed and gleamed on the windowsill, and all the life around it was transformed. Then on the seventh day it vanished. There was no trace of it to be found, though Ivan and Peter searched for it everywhere. But when Ivan looked at Peter's face he thought, "The lily glows there still." When they saw the clean pure house, and spoke with love to each other, and greeted their neighbors, and tended the growing things in the new garden, each thought to himself, "The lily still lives, though we see it no longer."

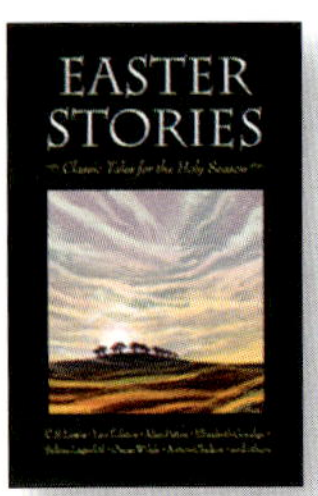

This story is taken from Easter Stories: Classic Tales for the Holy Season *(Plough, 2015).*

Hitler's Nemesis

My Battle against Hitler: Faith, Truth, and Defiance in the Shadow of the Third Reich, Dietrich von Hildebrand, ed. John Henry Crosby (Image, 352 pages)

"That damned Hildebrand is the greatest obstacle for National Socialism in Austria. No one causes more harm." With these words, Franz von Papen, the German ambassador to Austria, summed up with uncharacteristic insight the philosopher and theologian Dietrich von Hildebrand (1889–1977). In a confidential letter to Hitler, Papen labeled his fellow Catholic "the mastermind" of the Austrian intellectual resistance and suggested a plot to assassinate him. *My Battle against Hitler* tells the story of a man who dared, uncompromisingly, to follow his conscience in the face of seemingly unstoppable evil.

As his friends and acquaintances – many in high governmental and societal positions – became blinded or resigned to National Socialism's horrors, the philosopher Hildebrand retained his moral clarity and resolve. His fight against Nazism spanned at least two decades; already in 1923, while living in Munich, he learned he was on the Nazi blacklist for his outspoken rejection of nationalism and anti-Semitism. When Hitler seized power in 1933, Hildebrand fled to Italy and later settled in Austria, founding an anti-Nazi journal. Upon Germany's annexation of Austria in 1938, Hildebrand was forced to flee again, this time across Europe and then across the Atlantic, eventually arriving in New York in 1940. Throughout this odyssey, nothing – not the loss of personal property or the threat of death – could frighten him into silence. That is why his voice deserves to be heard today.

"From day one, his guideline was 'truth,'" his widow, Dr. Alice von Hildebrand, said in a recent interview. "On his deathbed he confided his whole literary bequest to me and he said, 'If you find anything which is not true, *burn it!*' That was his greatness. Truth is never 'mine.' It is ours. It is offered to all." This humility kept Hildebrand from publicizing his experiences when other resisters to Nazism became widely celebrated after World War II. But Alice, whom Hildebrand married after his first wife Gretchen died in 1957, begged him to write his memoirs.

Hildebrand's account makes up most of the book. In addition, excerpts from his essays reveal his methodical refutation of Nazi ideology and chart a philosophical road map for combating pervasive moral error.

Taken together, these writings are an essential witness to the power of a good conscience. Knowing he spoke the truth, Hildebrand possessed the rare freedom of those who know their cause will stand under the lens of the eternal. As he wrote to a former friend who – accepting the axiom *vox temporis, vox Dei* (the voice of the times is the voice of God) – had capitulated to Nazi ideology: "God calls us to fight the Antichrist regardless of whether we triumph, which ultimately is up to God. If God permits such evils as Bolshevism and National Socialism, then of course, as Saint Paul says, it is to test us; it is precisely our struggle against evil that God wills, even when we suffer external defeat."

Erna Albertz

READING

Growing into Manhood

PETER MOMMSEN

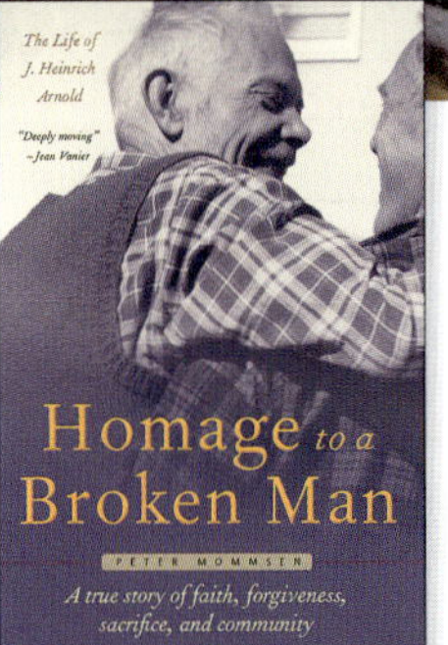

From *Homage to a Broken Man: The Life of J. Heinrich Arnold – A True Story of Faith, Forgiveness, Sacrifice, and Community* (Plough, 2015)

It's 1934, and Heiner is the twenty-year-old son of German theologian, revivalist, and pacifist Eberhard Arnold, the founder of the Bruderhof communities. Having fled Nazi Germany to escape military conscription, Heiner is now a teacher at the community's school in the Alpine Principality of Liechtenstein and madly in love with a fellow teacher, his future wife Annemarie. The political situation is growing more dangerous – the Nazis have infiltrated tiny Liechtenstein, and rumors swirl of illegal killings. But Heiner, formerly exuberant, is increasingly lost in an interior battle, oblivious of the evils threatening both his community and the continent at large. He struggles with doubts about his calling from God.

Heiner, around age twenty

Heiner was miserable, his world falling apart. He accused himself. How had he fallen so far from the faith of his childhood? Why had the fire that had flared in him at the time of his conversion died? For whole days at a time, he lost himself in morbid introspection. "I am a failure at everything, I can't be trusted with anything. I have no idea how to go on." He began to hate himself.

Eberhard noticed Heiner's gloom, and it disturbed him. His son seemed to believe that it was somehow meritorious to torment oneself. Perhaps he was trying to purge himself, or to prove his mettle. But it could not be allowed to go on – not if Heiner was his son. "When there is pus in the wound, it must be drawn out to heal." And so one evening during the course of a community meeting, he prodded Heiner to tell everyone what was on his mind.

Heiner rose and made the statement he had long been preparing. "I am co-guilty for everything wrong that has happened here. Because of my many mistakes, I am not fit to be involved in educational work. I ask to resign from the school."

Eberhard rose to his full height. "Heiner, you suffer from being in love with yourself. Do you think you are scoring points with God by continually talking about your failures? Our failure is a certainty to us, and so we go forward from it and get down to business. Your humble play-acting is not genuine. You are perverting your youthfulness. . . .

Heiner stood staring at his father with blank despair – he had known his father to shout, but never before like this. The circle of faces around him blurred, and only his father's remained clear.

"Heiner, go back to the starting point, just as if you were a child again. Is this the kind of person you wanted to be when you were eleven and so full of dreams for the future? Heiner and his little plans for a cozy marriage must disappear behind the big questions: What will become of the injustices all around us, which cry to heaven? What will become of Nazi Germany and Soviet Russia? What is your responsibility in the face of all this? You have a sound body and a sound soul; you have gifts and strength. Use

Photograph by Clare Stober

Photograph courtesy of the Bruderhof Archives

them! With your melancholy attitude you are living in chronic suicide.

"Why does success mean so much to you? It's putting on make-up before God. You think you are not doing well enough. Then you analyze yourself to find the cause of your guilt. You think you have to make yourself still humbler, to evoke God's pity. That is egoism! You want to make the Creator into your packhorse!"

In the silence that followed, the only sounds were the clock ticking and Eberhard's quick breath. Eberhard seemed to be waiting for something. Then he said, "Heiner, you have to recognize how utterly lost you are. What you said tonight comes from the abyss."

The meeting ended. Heiner was numb. As if through thick glass, he saw his father hobbling toward him, asking him, "How is it possible, Heiner?" His face was no longer angry so much as bewildered. "How is it possible that you let things go so far? Is this all we can expect from you after your childhood, after the Sun Troop, and after all we have experienced together? Why didn't you tell me what was going on here?" Heiner stood abjectly, saying nothing. His father pressed him. "Heiner, why are you like this?"

"That's just the way I am."

"What?" Eberhard cried out, his energy back in a flash. "Do you know what you are saying? You are accusing God! You're accusing your mother! You're accusing me!" The anguish in his father's face would haunt Heiner for the rest of his life.

Heiner began to tremble violently during the pause that followed. Then Eberhard said quietly and with deep sorrow, "You are the son in whom I had the greatest hope. And now you say this

Why We Need Stories Like *Homage to a Broken Man*

Adapted from the Foreword

As a pastor, I have spent most of my adult life looking for connections between the lives of those with whom I am living and the stories of the men and women I read about in the Bible. Just as the entire biblical revelation comes to us in the form of story, so today nothing less than great storytelling is adequate to render the intricacy of creation and redemption in our own lives.

Peter Mommsen's new biography of his grandfather, *Homage to a Broken Man,* tells a story worthy to take its place in the company of the "greatest story ever told," as an extension of that biblical story into the circumstances of our contemporary lives.

As I read this book, lines from Psalm 118 came to mind: "The stone that the builders rejected has become the cornerstone." Anticipating his imminent crucifixion, Jesus used these words to describe himself. It struck me as an apt text to describe the "broken man" of this story as well, a follower of Jesus who was also a "stone that the builders rejected." Another scripture this story will evoke, I must admit, is Jesus' counsel to his followers as he prepares them for what will most certainly come as they give witness to his new life of love and salvation: "One's foes will be members of one's own household" (Matt. 10:36).

Baron Friedrich von Hügel, the Austrian writer and theologian, was fond of saying, "There are no dittos among souls." At school I learned to marvel that no two snowflakes are alike, no two oak leaves identical. How much more unique is each human being! A true hearing of the gospel always

View of the Principality of Liechtenstein

Photograph by Reto Beer

takes in the specifically personal. "I have called you by name" (Isa. 43:1) has become an essential element both in my personal life and pastoral vocation.

Every time someone is addressed by name and realizes that in the encounter they are being treated as one-of-a-kind – not as a customer, not as a patient, not as a voter, not as a sinner – the gospel is served. Saving love is always personally specific, never merely generic. Christ's mercy is always customized to an individual, never swallowed up in an abstraction.

A good writer gives us eyes to see past the labels, ears to hear beneath stereotyping clichés. Peter Mommsen is such a writer. By the time you finish the book you will have made a new friend in Heinrich Arnold. In fact, this book introduces us to a whole cast of characters whose stories can heighten our own awareness and sensitivity to the life of Christ being lived in us.

Evil is not, as some think, the greatest mystery. The mysteries of goodness and redemption far exceed it, but they can be entered only when evil is faced. These mysteries become apparent when we find companions like those brought to life in the pages of this book, in communities like the Bruderhof and in unassuming and patient leaders like Heinrich Arnold.

Eugene H. Peterson, the author of over thirty books, is a scholar, poet, pastor, and translator of The Message: The Bible in Contemporary Language *(Navpress, 2002). He lives in Montana.*

to me?" Heiner could not answer. The two of them went out into the night, Eberhard on his crutches, along the footpath that ran from the chalet. Above the peaks stretched the vastness of a starry sky. Looking into the valley they could make out the faint line of the Rhine River three thousand feet below. The lights of the towns along its banks twinkled as if from another world. Suddenly Eberhard asked, "Have you ever thought of all the people who live down there, with all their loves and sufferings and sins? Have you ever asked yourself what meaning each of their lives ought to have? Have you ever thought of the day when God's rule will break over this earth, and each of the little houses in the valley will be flooded with light? Has any of this ever concerned you or disturbed you?"

Heiner answered. No, he had never really thought about this.

"Then where is your Christianity?" his father said sharply.

They stood side by side, gazing down. Heiner felt cold ripples up and down his neck. Gradually it dawned on him what it was all about. His father was saving him from something far worse than a life of failure or misery or even wickedness. He was saving him from choosing the comfort of pious complacency over a daring adventure. From denying his calling.

As Heiner recognized all this, he was filled with gratefulness. The strength of his father's love overwhelmed him. *(Continued in the book…)*

Richard John Neuhaus: A Life in the Public Square
Randy Boyagoda (Image)

This substantive new biography mines the mind of Neuhaus (1936–2009), one of the leading public intellectuals of the last half-century. From prominent antiwar cleric to outspoken conservative Catholic, the arc of Neuhaus's life might seem one of contradiction, but this volume, drawing heavily on his personal correspondence, reveals an authentic spiritual and intellectual striving to remain true to an ardent faith in Christ, as well as an uncommon capacity for friendship. Neuhaus's genius was to boldly engage people of every persuasion on many of the most pressing issues of his day. Evangelicals and Catholics Together (see page 7) and *First Things* magazine are two ongoing expressions of his legacy.

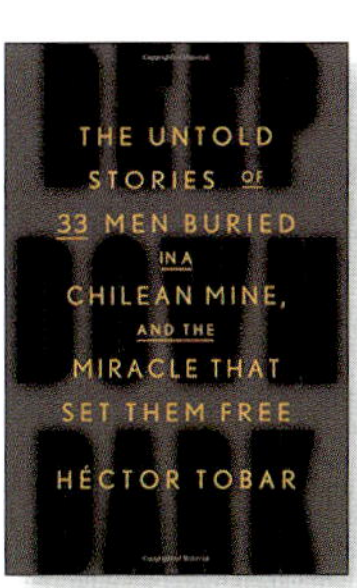

Deep Down Dark: The Untold Stories of 33 Men Buried in a Chilean Mine, and the Miracle That Set Them Free
Héctor Tobar
(Farrar, Straus and Giroux)

Based on exclusive interviews with the survivors of the 2010 Chilean mining disaster, this riveting account is a memorable exploration of human nature – and the uncanny power of brotherly affection. Trapped as much by their fear of dying as by two thousand vertical feet of rock, the miners endured hunger, thirst, and near-despair before an enormous drill bit reached them. But it's unlikely they could have emerged intact had it not been for their faith in the power of prayer and their willingness to put aside differences for the sake of the common good. Tobar, a Pulitzer Prize–winning journalist, takes us not only down into the stifling underworld the miners inhabit, but also into the heart of a remarkable ad hoc community which saved its members just as surely as the capsule that hauled them to the surface after their ten-week nightmare underground.

Black River: A Novel
S. M. Hulse
(Houghton Mifflin Harcourt)

When Wes Carver, a Montana correctional officer, was maimed by a prisoner during a riot twenty years ago, he lost his greatest gift: an uncommon ability to play the fiddle. Now the man is up for parole, and Wes has been asked to testify at the hearing. While billed as a story of forgiveness, faith, and family, it's more accurately about the inability to forgive, the elusiveness of faith, and the long odds of restoring wounded psyches and tattered relationships. This is one debut novel that lives up to the acclaim: the characters are convincing, the details are authentic, and the storyline is captivating to the very last page.

Change of Heart: Justice, Mercy, and Making Peace with My Sister's Killer
Jeanne Bishop
(Westminster John Knox)

Defense attorney Jeanne Bishop ventures beyond forgiveness in this candid, compelling memoir of her journey to reach out to a man who had killed her sister when he was fifteen. What do justice and mercy demand? Can we believe that God wants to bring about not only closure but even reconciliation and restoration? Bishop is straightforward about her own transformation, which didn't happen all at once and never would have come about without help from others along the way, including her own young children. *The Editors*

From WikiArt (public domain)

Master of the Winking Eyes, *Madonna and Child,* tempera and gold on wood panel, Grimaldi Fava Collection, Cento, Italy

Meeting Mary

HOWARD BUSKIRK

The Holy Mother is playfully gripping the baby Jesus while she gazes directly at the viewer with smiling eyes, as if to share her joy. Her humanity shines from this tempera and gold painting by the unnamed "Master of the Winking Eyes." This is one of sixty depictions of Mary in *Picturing Mary: Woman, Mother, Idea,* an exhibit at the National Museum of Women in the Arts (NMWA) that traces artistic portrayals of Mary from the thirteenth to the nineteenth century. Developed in partnership with the Catholic University of America, the exhibit will not travel from the NMWA, which is remarkable given the jewel box of art works it

Picturing Mary: Woman, Mother, Idea, National Museum of Women in the Arts (NMWA), Washington, DC, December 5, 2014–April 12, 2015, *www.nmwa.org*

From WikiArt (public domain)

Lorenzo di Credi, *The Annunciation,* tempera on wood panel, Galleria degli Uffizi, Florence

includes, many shown in the United States for the first time.

The works demonstrate a broad range of media – paintings, prints, ceramics, and wood carvings – to depict the great moments in Mary's life, ranging from Lorenzo di Credi's *Annunciation* and Fra Lippi's luminescent *Madonna and Child* to Maison Samson's heartrending *Deposition from the Cross* to Rembrandt's drawing *Death of the Virgin* and Dürer's *Assumption.*

The exhibit is heavy on Renaissance and Baroque works, notably a Vasari *Crucifixion* and an exquisite small tempera by Botticelli. Outstanding is Caravaggio's *Rest on the Flight into Egypt,* painted by the artist in his early twenties. The work shows the baby Jesus and Mary asleep, while an angel stands, his winged back to the viewer, playing violin from a score held by Joseph. Although this early work does not display the dramatic light study for which Caravaggio is famous, it is nonetheless important as one of his first large canvases.

From Michelangelo there is a single drawing in red and black chalk, on loan from the Casa Buonarroti in Florence. In this *Madonna and Child,* Mary looks alertly up at something in the distance. Only the arm of the baby Jesus is fully executed, but the other details are vivid, drawn with the deft line that distinguishes Michelangelo's work. This is a flesh-and-blood Mary with the liveliness of the figures in the Sistine Chapel.

Since the Reformation, Westerners' attitudes to Mary have too often been polarized: she is attacked or defended as a sign of division between Catholics and Protestants. *Picturing Mary* helps us recover the real Mary – not a polemical symbol but a real woman of history, one whose relationship to Jesus remains forever unique. This exhibit provides a beautiful door through which to meet the very human Mother of God.

Howard Buskirk is a journalist and executive senior editor of Communications Daily.

Johnny Appleseed

Veery Huleatt

In 1829, as a wave of revivals swept America, a preacher addressed a crowd in Mansfield, Ohio. He challenged them: "Where now is your barefooted pilgrim on his way to heaven?"

"Here he is." A man stepped forward, barefoot and wearing a coffee sack for a shirt. He was John Chapman (1774–1845), a man who lived on the American frontier, planting apple orchards and bearing "good news fresh from heaven" and a name that would become American folk legend: Johnny Appleseed.

Chapman was an apple nurseryman, starting orchards in plots of land that could then be settled and cultivated. Although his business was apparently successful – he owned 1,200 acres at his death – he never left his rough and solitary way of life. Chapman's diet of honey, wild berries, milk, and cornmeal was reminiscent of John the Baptist's. He had his namesake's zeal as well; once when he came across a woman throwing out food he admonished her, telling her that "it was a violation of the gifts of a merciful God."

But Chapman is most remembered for his kindness. He gave apple seedlings to people too poor to purchase them, and one winter he gave his only pair of shoes to a family travelling west. Chapman extended this kindness to all creatures, even snakes and insects, and earned the respect of the Native American tribes he encountered. His reverence for nature went further than many of his contemporaries thought was sensible. He felt that grafting – the preferred method of propagating fruit trees, in which scions from good varieties are grafted onto a hardy rootstock – was a trespass of the Creator's work. The apples from the trees he planted were therefore unsuitable for eating; their primary use was hard cider and apple jack.

Chapman carried a Bible at all times, as well as the writings of Emanuel Swedenborg, the Swedish religious writer who influenced thinkers from William Blake to Ralph Waldo Emerson. He spent many nights sleeping by strangers' hearths, and on such occasions Chapman often read the Sermon on the Mount to his hosts. His selfless kindness showed how earnestly he sought to live by its precepts.

Today Chapman would probably be institutionalized as insane, but the wilderness and the rough times he lived in had room for his idiosyncrasies. While adults called him crazy, citing a story that he had been kicked in the head by a horse as a young man, children looked forward to his visits. Chapman enjoyed their company, bringing ribbons for the girls and reportedly entertaining the boys by walking barefooted over burning coals.

He was a man seen in glimpses, leaving only a scattering of reliable records. This was fertile ground for legend, and the Johnny Appleseed we know today has far outgrown the original John Chapman. In this case, the truth may be more marvelous than the myth. As N. N. Hill, an Ohio historian, wrote in 1881, "Not once in a century is such a life of self-sacrifice for the good of others known."

To get to know the real John Chapman, see Howard B. Means's fascinating Johnny Appleseed: The Man, the Myth, the American Story *(Simon and Schuster, 2011). This article draws on Means's research.*